NEW PARISH MINISTERS

Laity & Religious on Parish Staffs

A study conducted for the
Committee on Pastoral Practices
of the
National Conference of Catholic Bishops
with the support of Lilly Endowment, Inc.

Philip J. Murnion

with David DeLambo, Rosemary Dilli, S.S.N.D., Harry A. Fagan

National Pastoral Life Center

Printed in the United States of America

The director of this research project was Philip J. Murnion; Coordinator: Rosemary Dilli,
S.S.N.D.; principal data analyst: David DeLambo; coordinator of on-site visits: Harry A.
Fagan; word processing: Cathy Katoski, O.S.F. Also assisting: Mary Good, Theresa
Fahey, R.S.H.M., and Maureen McKenna M.H.S.H., Book designer: Emil Antonucci.
Editor: Karen Sue Smith.

ISBN: 1-881307-01-8

TABLE OF CONTENTS

LIST OF CHARTS AND TABLES

Study Summary

About 20,000 lay people and religious are employed at least twenty hours a week as parish ministers in half the 19,000 Catholic parishes of the United States. This is in addition to those on the staffs of the parochial schools and those in support or maintenance positions. The number represents a dramatic change from a generation ago when there were few such parish ministers other than the organists or music directors or the parish visitors in mission areas; the priests took care of parish ministry.

This is among the findings of a study undertaken by the National Pastoral Life Center at the request of the Committee on Pastoral Practices of the National Conference of Catholics Bishops. The study was funded by Lilly Endowment of Indianapolis. The report draws on results from: an initial survey of 2198 parishes randomly chosen from forty-three dioceses, follow-up surveys of 655 parishes (their staffs and parishioners), and site visits in fifty-two parishes.

Eighty-five percent of the new parish ministers are women and fifteen percent are men. Slightly more than four out of ten are members of religious orders, the vast majority sisters and relatively few brothers; almost six in ten are lay people. All together, these are a very well-educated group, more than half with a master's degree, and the religious among them are even more educated with 80 percent possessing a master's degree.

The religious tend to be considerably older than the lay people: 40 percent of the religious are over sixty years of age, while only 8 percent of the lay people are that old. The future will apparently mean more lay people on parish staffs and, unless there are significant changes, it will also mean a somewhat less educated group and one with somewhat less education in Catholic schools as well. The religious average between thirteen and fourteen years of Catholic schooling while the lay people average ten and two-thirds years. Furthermore, the younger lay ministers--those under thirty-five--average just fewer than nine years.

While most of the new parish ministers think that they are well prepared in the areas of theology and ministry (and their pastors agree), a significant number indicate that they wish they had been better grounded in doctrinal and moral theology, in Sacred Scripture and liturgy, as well as in some of the skills necessary for parish life, viz. counselling, supervising, and handling conflict.

Contrary to the fears sometimes expressed that adding laity and religious to parish staffs might usurp the responsibilities of the parishioners themselves, the study finds that these ministers actually increase the involvement of parishioners in parish life. Further, there is no evidence that the presence of a parochial school lessens parishes' ability to pay for additional ministers, except in smaller and poorer parishes, which are less likely than other parishes to have these new staff members.

The parish ministry that has led the way in this development has been religious education, which currently accounts for four out of ten parish ministers. The next largest group are those in general parish ministry positions called "pastoral associates," "pastoral assistants," "parish ministers," or some similar title. This is a growing segment of the ministry group, now accounting for over 27 percent of the total. Next come music ministers (7.8 percent), youth ministers (7.5 percent), and those responsible for parish liturgy and catechumenate (about 5 percent). The remaining ministers are responsible for many different concerns such as the elderly, the sick, social ministry, spirituality, or evangelization. A small percentage, in this study less than one percent, are "parish administrators," people who are responsible for the ongoing ministry of a parish in the absence of a resident priest. Though other studies suggest a larger number of people in these positions, the results of this study indicate that somewhat fewer than 200 lay people or religious are acting as parish administrators.

The study was intended to determine not only what is happening regarding lay people and religious in parish ministry but how well it is going. By everyone's measure--those of the ministers themselves, the pastors in these parishes, the other ordained priests and deacons, and parishioners--things are going very well indeed. The vast majority of the lay ministers are quite satisfied with their situations and all feel that these ministers have made a significant contribution to parish life. They have improved the parishes' educational, liturgical, and social ministries, broadening the parishes' reach to parishioners and especially to women. The ministers who experience the greatest difficulties and among whom there is more dissatisfaction are the youth ministers, musicians, and liturgists.

The majority of pastors have worked with the new ministers in establishing job descriptions, scheduling staff meetings, and developing other means of sharing communication and authority that make for good working relationships. Such formal means of cooperating in ministry, however, need further development. Of even greater concern are the interactions between pastor and parish minister that are more personal: performance reviews and reactions to one another's work.

Making room for the new parish ministers in both the budget and the buildings of parishes has not always been easy. Gradually, accommodations are being made. The average yearly salary ranges from $13,000 to $20,000 for full-time ministers, which a significant number of both the lay persons and the religious say is a problem for meeting their own needs and those of their families (of lay persons) and their congregations (of the religious). Low salaries may have the greatest negative influence on long-term commitments to parish ministry.

Which themes are especially strong in the development of parish ministry? First, the shift in personnel introduces a strong lay dimension to parish ministry with all the distinct needs and sensibilities that lay people bring to it. Second, the new parish ministers add a strong feminine dimension to parish ministry, both in the presence of women on staffs and in the attention to relationships as well as tasks that women typically bring to the work place. Third, the emergence of lay ministry has had a sharply local quality, with all the advantages and disadvantages this brings-- establishing positions, their responsibilities and requirements, has been largely determined by pastors and increasingly means hiring parishioners. Fourth, the shift in who ministers suggests that ministry is not inevitably linked to one's state of life (vowed or ordained vs. lay) nor to one's professional certification; ministry is a category of its own combining skills and relationships. Fifth, parishes and dioceses are adopting personnel policies and practices to ensure just and adequate treatment of church workers which will protect both the ministers and the ministry. Finally, the number of African-American and Hispanic ministers is very low, totaling less than five percent of all the lay and religious parish ministers.

The study suggests that among the areas warranting attention are: the theological and ministerial preparation of the increasingly lay parish staff members; more assurance of proper personnel procedures; efforts to provide adequate salaries and stipends; preparation of pastors for the new relationships required with staff members; attention to the overly "parochial" quality of ministers who come from among the parishioners; the often strained relationships of pastors with music, liturgy, and youth ministers; greater diocesan involvement in this ministerial development without diminishing parish initiative or adaptations.

Introduction

The present study began with a request addressed by Bishop Timothy Harrington of Worcester to the annual meeting of the National Conference of Catholic Bishops in November, 1988. Bishop Harrington urged a study of lay people in the church from a variety of perspectives. His request was assigned to the Pastoral Research and Practices Committee from which a subcommittee was formed, originally chaired by Bishop Robert Carlson, auxiliary of St. Paul-Minneapolis, which consulted with numerous people in order to establish a focus for the study. After considerable discussion, the committee, then chaired by Bishop James Hoffman, determined that there was a need to examine the rapidly expanding practice of hiring lay people and religious for pastoral positions in parishes. Since, canonically, religious are lay as distinct from clergy one could properly use the term "lay parish ministers" to denote the subjects of the study, but for the sake of clarity we will refer to lay and religious pastoral ministers.

While religious and laity had long been central to parish school faculties, the past generation has seen them take parish positions concerned with religious education, youth, social service, elderly, liturgy, music, and other pastoral ministries. It was the committee's interest to learn what factors are fostering this practice, what obstacles limit it, what conditions seem helpful and what seem harmful to the good of parish ministry and that of these parish ministers themselves. The study was originally restricted to lay persons and religious serving full time in parishes in pastoral (vs. support) positions, other than on school faculties. Early on, this was expanded to include part-time personnel who were employed to work at least twenty hours, because we felt that this was necessary to capture some ministries (such as music) where the arrangement is often for part-time service.

The committee agreed to a study plan proposed by the National Pastoral Life Center. The Center was then engaged by the committee to carry out this plan. The Center was to conduct the study and deliver a report to the committee which will then determine what actions it might recommend to the body of bishops as a result of the study. Funding for the study was sought and obtained from Lilly Endowment, Inc. of Indianapolis as part of the Endowment's general interest in leadership issues in the Catholic Church. The study was then begun in December 1989.

Organization of the Study

The study process drew on the various dimensions of the National Pastoral Life Center, its research capacity, its contact through its publications and regional parish ministry conventions with those concerned about parish ministry, its linkage with dioceses through consultations, conferences and monthly teleconferences over CTNA, and its contact with academic and ministry formation centers.

The study structure has had five parts:

1. Review of the results of earlier studies

2. A variety of consultations:
   A. some that helped to **shape the study**:
      1) use of one of the National Pastoral Life Center teleconferences conducted by satellite over CTNA which solicited advice through telephone call-ins and through forms distributed at over 70 diocesan sites throughout the country
      2) consultations with a few hundred lay and religious parish ministers as well as pastors and active parishioners assembled for National Pastoral Life Center parish ministry conventions in St. Louis and Cleveland
   B. some that helped to **understand and interpret findings**: with diocesan offices related to lay ministry, with directors of ministry training and formation centers and programs, with representatives of various kinds of ministers (religious education, youth, etc.) that provided expert information

3. A survey (Phase I) of a sample of parishes in the dioceses randomly selected in all of the 13 NCCB regions of the country to determine basic composition and characteristics of the parishes as well as both the staffing patterns and the specific names of lay persons, religious, pastors and other ordained ministers who are in the parishes.

4. A survey (Phase II) of those parishes with lay and religious parish ministers that involved four distinct survey forms:
   A. a survey instrument for each lay and religious parish minister in the sample parishes
   B. a survey instrument for the pastor
   C. a survey instrument for each of the ordained parochial vicars and deacons in the parishes
   D. survey instruments to be distributed to five well-informed parishioners in each of the sample parishes, preferably those elected to serve on parish pastoral or finance councils or who are otherwise well informed about the workings of the individual parish ministers

5. On-site visits to 52 parishes selected to reflect as well as one can with such a small number the types of parishes that emerged from the first phase of the study (attentive to distinctions such as locale--urban, suburban, rural, etc--size, presence or absence of school, etc.). To reflect the nation, we chose two dioceses in each of the thirteen NCCB regions of the country, and two parishes in each of these dioceses. In each parish we visited, our observer interviewed all the parish ministers, the pastor and others on staff, and a selection of parishioners. The observers also had a chance to observe the parish staff in action, sometimes at staff meetings, and in some instances to meet with the parish pastoral council.

The following summarizes the numbers of parishes, pastoral ministers, and parishioners contacted by means of the Phase I and Phase II surveys and the site visits.

SURVEY SAMPLES AND RETURNS AND SITE VISIT CONTACTS

Phase One: Parish Survey

Sample dioceses	43	
Sample parishes	2198	(about 40 pct.)
Returns No.	1163	
Percent	52.9	

Phase Two: Minister Survey

		Returns	
	Surveyed	No.	Pct.
Pastors	655	510	77.9
Lay/Religious	1368	982	71.8
Other Staff	529	340	64.3
Parishioners	3240	1905	58.8

Phase Three: Site Visits and Interviews

Parishes	52 (2x26 dioceses)
Pastors	52
Lay/Religious	118
Other Staff	34
Parishioners	208 (4x52)

The study design was intended to assemble a rich mix of information: a reliable profile of the nation's parishes via the probability sample of parishes and their ministers; the nuances and illustrations of the reality captured by the survey statistics that can come only from direct observation and communication with those involved;

the experience and interpretive insights of those who are related to the phenomenon from a variety of positions; the learnings of other studies which both helped focus elements of this study and provided a base against which to compare the results of this study. The intent and method was to be both systematic (carefully chosen sample of all parishes) and strategic (consulting those who have particularly instructive experience with some aspects of the matters we were studying).

Regarding the original sample, we had the assistance of both Rev. James Mahoney, a consultant to the early stages of the project, and a sampling expert from National Opinion Research Center. As a result we originally selected 30 dioceses, oversampling the regions with more dioceses. When we reviewed the first returns, we determined that the whole number of lay and religious parish ministers might not be adequate for analysis and added another 13 dioceses to the sample. In each diocese we drew a sample of about 40 percent of the parishes.

The Phase I questionnaire was necessarily rather lengthy, for this would be our only contact with those parishes that did *not* have any lay or religious parish ministers. The information gathered through this survey would enable us to compare the parishes with and without such ministers in order to identify the contextual or environmental factors that seem to influence staffing patterns. These include parish size, income, parishioner composition, locale (e.g. urban, rural), clergy staffing, complexity of ministries, presence or absence of a school and its costs to the parish, region of the country and the like. As a result, the forms were rather taxing to complete. Nonetheless, we feel that the returns from this Phase I mailing, the distribution of whose parishes by locale, size, and region well match the pattern found in other studies, are adequate to draw conclusions.

Comparing the profile of parishes in the returns from Phase I survey with that in the Notre Dame Study of Catholic Parish Life indicates a close match in terms of parish size and locale. The present study has a slightly higher percentage of rural/resort parishes and a slightly lower percentage of suburban/exurban and urban parishes, but the differences are not significant.

LOCALE OF PARISHES IN PHASE I RETURNS
Compared with Profile from Notre Dame Study[1]

Locale	Present Study %	Notre Dame Study %
Inner City	11	14
Business	4	3
Other Urban	13	13
Suburban/Exurban	19	24
Small Town	30	32
Rural/Resort	22	14

PARISH SIZE IN PHASE I RETURNS
Compared with Profile from Notre Dame Study[2]

Number of Parishioners	Present Study %	Notre Dame Study %
Fewer than 500	19	18
500-999	17	17
1,000-1,499	11	12
1,500-2,499	15	13
2,500-4,999	19	21
5,000-9,999	10	12
10,000 or more	9	5

For Phase II, we did not select a sample from the parishes contacted through the first phase survey. Instead, we sent survey forms to all the parishes that returned their questionnaires and that had paid lay and religious parish ministers employed for twenty or more hours a week. The letter accompanying the survey forms asked the pastor to distribute the respective forms to the lay and religious parish ministers and the other ordained ministers (as identified on each form) and to the parishioners in the manner we indicated. We provided separate return envelopes for each person to return those survey forms directly to the researchers. The returns from this mailing were quite good, more than three-quarters of the pastors and almost as many of the lay and religious parish ministers. (Frankly we had anticipated that the highest rate of returns would come from the lay and religious ministers.) The other staff returns are quite good as well. Regarding the parishioner returns, we have reason to believe that all the pastors did not in fact distribute all five survey forms, which would account for the lower percentage of returns. The site visits were conducted by members of the National Pastoral Life Center staff and adjunct staff recruited for this purpose. Each visitor spent three or four days in a diocese (in some instances the visitor already lived in that diocese and could spend more time and had other sources of information about the parish) and divided their time between the two parishes to be visited and some diocesan staff who were consulted.

All who visited these parishes were deeply impressed by the experience. None of the parishes chosen rejected our phone request to make a visit. The visitors were shown almost unfailing hospitality and extraordinary confidence and trust in the interviews. The parish staffs and parishioners were usually very grateful for the visit, appreciative that the bishops wished to hear from them and to learn from their experience. In most instances, the visit served as affirmation of their efforts. These visits more than fulfilled our hopes to put "flesh and blood" on the bones of the statistics from the survey. This will be evident throughout the report, by our ability to interpret and illustrate the findings from the surveys with examples from the site visits.

The combination of what the social researchers call quantitative research (the survey research) with qualitative research (the site visits, interviews with expert informants, and examination of certain strategic examples) enriches our study. **In reporting our findings, however, we will try to distinguish among these sources of insight, by presenting in italics the learnings from the qualitative research.**

This report of the study is offered to all concerned with parish ministry in the United States with the hope that it may help us to understand what has happened in the past generation and help us to take the steps necessary for the next generation. While the research team has deliberately resisted concluding the report with lists of specific recommendations, settling rather for drawing together some significant conclusions, it will be the task of the sponsoring NCCB committee and those in positions of leadership in dioceses and other related church institutions to formulate recommendations and appropriate actions they think ensue from what we have learned.

Acknowledgments

I would like to acknowledge all of those who have participated in any way in this study. These include our own study staff, the sponsoring and advisory committee, auxiliary staff and consultants.

The National Pastoral Life Center staff for the study included Rev. Philip J. Murnion, Sr. Rosemary Dilli, SSND, coordinator of the project, Mr. David De Lambo, Mr. Harry Fagan, Sr. Cathy Katoski, OSF, and Sr. Maureen McKenna, MHSH. David De Lambo, the Center's research analyst, was primarily responsible for orchestrating the programing and statistical analysis of the data. Others on the Center staff were all engaged in the project in some way. These include the editor of the report Ms. Karen Sue Smith, Ms. Mary Good, Mr. Lawrence Becker, Sr. Theresa Fahey, RSHM, Mr. Tino Torres, and our producer for teleconferences, Rev. James Gardiner, SA. Rev. James Mahoney served as survey consultant in the early stages of the project. Our computer consultant, Mr. Edward Smith, provided important assistance. A student of mine, Jane Dwyer, assisted us in doing an analysis of the job descriptions submitted by the lay ministers completing the survey. We also drew on a number of students for data entry and are grateful to them.

In addition to staff of the National Pastoral Life Center eight persons assisted us in undertaking the site visitations: Mrs. Judith Kollar, Sister Catherine Lee, CSJ, Ms. Mary Baudouin, Mrs. Mary Tardiff, Mr. Stephen Rall, Ms. Patricia Lewis, Mr. George Noonan, and Mrs. Rochelle Pearl Koller. This team of visitors not only provided very useful reports of their observations, but a number of them were able to attend a session with our advisory group at which we reflected on the findings; in this they also proved to be very helpful interpreters.

The study had the benefit of advice from many others. First, the bishops' subcommittee for the project and their consultants were helpful in establishing a focus for the study. This committee was chaired by the Most Reverend James R. Hoffman. Representing the Committee on Priestly Life and Ministry was the Most Reverend John A. Marshall; representing the Committee on the Laity was the Most Reverend Raymond A. Lucker. This committee's consultants were Mrs. Dolores Leckey, Mr. H. Richard McCord, Ms. Zeni Fox, Reverend David Brinkmoeller, and Reverend Maurice Monnette. Father Michael Walsh, staff to the Pastoral Research and Practices Committee of the NCCB was our liaison and served perfectly in that capacity, providing us all the support and freedom we needed for the project.

Second, the National Pastoral Life Center established its own advisory committee to perform three functions: to help determine the content of the study, to advise us of key informants regarding the subject of the study, and to help us interpret the findings. These persons proved enormously helpful to the study but are not responsible for any failings in the study or our report. The members of this advisory committee who were able to participate were: Sister Margaret Althisar, OP, Mr. Leonard Anguiano, Reverend J. Kevin Boland, Sister Louise Bond, SNJM, Sister Helen Marie Burns, RSM, Ms. Zoila Diaz, Ms. Virginia Sullivan Finn, Reverend Virgil C. Funk, Ms. Greer G. Gordon, Ms. Patricia S. Gries, Ms. Jean Marie Hiesberger, Sister Roalie Murphy, SND, Mr. Steve Rall, Mr. John Reid, Mr. John Roberto, Mr. Wayne F. Smith, Brother Loughlan Sofield, ST, Sister Mary Mark Tacheny, Ms. Joanne Welter, Sister Lea Woll, SLW.

Third, the study benefitted from a consulting session with Dr. Dean Hoge of Catholic University, Dr. Ruth Wallace of George Washington University, and Dr. James R. Kelly of Fordham University.

Fourth, we were able to draw on the insights of numerous people in diocesan offices and ministry formation schools.

But our greatest appreciation must go to all the pastors, pastoral ministers, and parishioners who were so generous and cooperative with the project. Obviously, it was their lives we were studying and we needed their permission and trust if the study were to be possible. This was true of both those in parishes where laity and religious were part of the staff and those where there were no lay ministers; in the latter instances the results of the study would be less pertinent. The admiration we have for these parish personnel will be evident in the pages that follow, but our appreciation for their cooperation cannot be measured.

We are grateful to Lilly Endowment and Mr. Fred Hofheinz, for the grant to the National Conference of Catholic Bishops for this project. The Endowment has been an invaluable supporter of research concerning ministry and leadership in the Catholic Church.

Finally, this report represents the work and views of the National Pastoral Life Center and not necessarily those of the National Conference of Catholic Bishops' committee or any of our consultants. We are grateful for the opportunity to cooperate with the bishops' committee in this way and hope that we will have served well both them and those in parishes who are working hard to meet today's pastoral needs.

Reverend Philip J. Murnion
Director, National Pastoral Life Center

I: New Patterns of Parish Ministry: Major Themes

The story we have to tell is one of amazingly inventive and pragmatic pastoral ministry. It is the story of how the church in the United States has found ways to meet new demands for parish community and mission in new circumstances. These new approaches are at once adaptive enough to cultural trends to be relevant and countercultural enough to protect the integrity of the church. It is also a story of how the church has richly benefitted from the sacrifices and achievements of the past. For what has happened has depended on all the strengths with which the church entered the last third of the twentieth century, the period after Vatican II. These include the work, primarily of religious orders, that established the Catholic colleges and universities which provided higher education specifically within the Catholic context to so many men and women, as well as the families that availed themselves of, and helped to pay for, these schools. For the shifts in pastoral ministry we are documenting have depended on the availability of significant numbers of lay people and religious with strong foundations in Catholic theology and culture. The Catholic universities played another important role, that of educating and certifying people for religious education, which was the first role in the broadening of parish ministry.

At this point, we would like to sketch the broad contours of what has happened, leaving the specific measures and more complex analyses for the most part to the chapters that follow.

This story is about a virtual revolution in pastoral ministry. A generation ago, almost all Catholic parish ministers, those who were formally part of the staff of a parish were priests, except for the sisters who administered and taught in the schools and parish visitors and catechists in some mission areas. (From here on, when we talk of parish staffs we are talking about those who are not part of the school staff.) A generation later, half of the parishes in the United States have lay people or religious in paid pastoral staff positions. Based on projections from our sample, it would appear that there are now about twenty thousand paid lay and religious pastoral ministers.

Since the ministers of the past were all priests, obviously they were all men. Now, 85 percent of the lay persons and religious on parish staffs, are women. Furthermore, somewhat less than half are sisters and of the lay women two-thirds are married. Added to the perspectives brought to parish ministry are those of women and men religious, single women, and married women, as well as those of lay men.

It would be a mistake to think that these trends affect only those parishes with paid lay/religious staffs. For even among the half of parishes which, largely because they are too small or have too little money, have not hired staff, the parishioners exercising leadership in their ministry are increasingly married and single lay women, as the Notre Dame Study of Catholic Parish Life has documented.

As a beginning to our report, we would like to distill some basic themes in this development. The revolution in ministry has meant parishes with stronger **lay**, **feminine**, **local**, and **ministerial** dimensions. A word about each.

A Lay Dimension

The lay dimension is evident from what we have already noted. Even if we distinguish among the new parish ministers those who are truly lay--not in religious vows--there are thousands of lay people now exercising formal pastoral ministry in parishes. Whether single or married, they bring a different set of perspectives and conditions of life to the exercise of ministry than do priests or religious.[3]

But an increasing lay dimension of parish life is to be found not only in the presence of lay people in parish ministry positions. It can also be found in the growing influence of lay persons on parish councils in shaping the priorities of the parish and even in selecting the staff for a parish.[4]

In this respect, the lay dimension denotes another change as well. Parish councils working with inventive parish priests and other pastoral ministers have broadened the reach of ministry beyond the more institutional frameworks of yesterday's ministry-- the sacraments and schools--to meet the new needs of today's parishioners. These new needs include support and sociability among the elderly and young adults, advocacy and organizing among the poor and near poor, healing groups for the bereaved and the separated and divorced.

Some commentators and church leaders have warned against the danger of "clericalizing" the laity. Apparently, that could happen if the church leaders show more concern for incorporating lay persons into the formal ministries of the church and into the "culture" of ministry, than in encouraging the specifically "lay" vocation "in the world." If pastoral ministry gives inadequate support to people's attempts to live the Christian life in their families, communities, and work places, as well as in our lives as citizens and consumers, this ministry does give short shrift to what has been called in the past the "apostolate of the laity." Furthermore, to the extent that parishes do this by preoccupation with parishioners' involvement in parish activities, they can seriously neglect the lay mission in the wider world.

But "clericalizing" can also occur if even the lay sensibilities of those working in church ministries are underemphasized or lost, and these lay ministers assume positions more and more like those of the vowed religious or ordained ministers.

We cannot document whether or not the employment of lay people in parish ministry positions has distracted these parishes from helping lay people in their mission "in the world." When it comes to the employment of lay people in positions of church ministry, it might be argued that the danger is not one of overly clericalizing them but of insufficiently "clericalizing" their status, that is, of insufficiently providing the formation, support, and integration of these ministers into the ministerial community of the church. For the situation of these ministers is decidedly lay in the sense that they do not live a life enclosed within the structures of ordination or vows, freely take and leave their positions, as one would a job, and are freely hired and fired by pastors without respect for their continuing in any role in ministry. On the other hand, the lay ministers often carry precisely their lay sensibilities into ministry, since all report that, as a group, they have enhanced parishes' sensitivity to lay concerns, those of family, of the elderly, and of women in general. Yet, to leave such a rapidly expanding number of people who will spend their lives in formal church ministry without the context of some "order" or officially structured ministry may not be enough to ensure adequate protection for either the ministers or the ministry.

Whatever happens in the future, at present the lay dimension of formal parish leadership has been markedly increased.

A Feminine Dimension

The changes in parish ministry have also had a decidedly feminine dimension. Again, this is not just a matter of how many women are now in formal positions of parish ministry, though this is of enormous importance. It relates to another aspect of the feminine dimension: the extent to which parishes are engaged in the kinds of support and nurturing activities that have been characteristically associated with women and with the church. Although there were always nurturing and supportive activities in parishes, parishes in the past could be viewed as empowering community organizations. Parish priests built the churches and schools, ministered to the sick (in situations more risky than today, because they were ministering to people at home with more communicable diseases), and mobilized the men of the parish into mutually supportive men's clubs and St. Vincent de Paul Societies, and young men and their fathers into sports teams.[5]

The situation of the present is decidedly different in the majority of parishes which are middle class. The parishioners do not need the parish as a base of power; they do not need or use the schools as a foundation for entering the society; the men do not gather in the parishes for support and fraternity; and the sick--who less often have contagious diseases anyway--have been removed to hospital care. Now the parish is caring for the young and the old, for the teenagers and those who are homebound. It is not surprising that a significant majority of the new ministers report that one of their responsibilities is home visiting. These parishes are rarely building as they once were. The parish is also not so much trying to provide firm teaching and discipline that will earn the parishioners a place not only in heaven but in responsible positions of society, as it is offering the kinds of small group experiences of prayer and discussion that allow them to feel support for their own achievements and concerns--Bible groups, prayer groups, separated and divorced groups, RENEW groups and the like. It is not authority that is entailed here but understanding and empathy. It is in these terms that we may speak about feminizing as a matter not only of the gender of the minsters but also of the orientation of the ministry. Of course, the matter may well be viewed from the other side, namely as a problem men have in our culture in responding to these opportunities for more personal engagement in the life of a community of faith.

The connection between the increasing female cast of the parish staff and the increasingly nurturing quality of parish life is evident enough, but this feminizing impact of the parish becomes more pronounced when we find that of all the possible contributions these ministers could make to parishioners, the ones that the ministers-- whether they are women or men--feel least confident of providing are both sensitivity to men's concerns and the involvement of men in the active life of the parish community. And parishes have yet to become adept at enabling parishioners who hold paid jobs--women as well as men--to reflect on the linkages between their faith and work, or to find in the community of faith encouragement for creativity and integrity in their occupations.

We cannot restrict our discussion of the feminine dimension of ministry to these consequences. Other developments in this respect are very important as well. For all of our convictions that developments in the church have a doctrinal or theological origin, we have to acknowledge the extent to which we are also affected by broader social and cultural trends. The challenge is to discern which trends the Spirit is using to lead the church and which trends are leading us away from authentic church life. That is not so easy. But, just as the church's adoption of councils and other forums to broaden consultation and participation in decision making was of a piece with similar developments of more participatory governance throughout Western culture, so the increasing role of women (and we might add the increasingly feminine character of the church in the broader sense) is of a piece with the broadening participation of women in social roles. With that development, especially to the extent that it is unplanned, can come both anomalies and tensions. These occur not only when certain roles and activities are denied women but also when this occurs while other ostensibly more important roles are opened to women.

There is one further way in which ministry is being feminized and that is in the relationships among those who are engaged in ministry. Many women who are in parish ministry come with expectations or hopes that they and the pastors and others in parish ministry will not just carry out their independent tasks, but will enjoy collaboration. Such collaboration calls for staff meetings, opportunities for sharing faith, and at least some occasions for socializing and looking to long-range dreams and plans. It is the relationships among those working together (as well as the work itself) that are important to these women.[6] To call this feminizing is not to say that only women call for this, though they are likely to place greater emphasis on these relationships than do most priests. Yet, increasingly priests themselves are introducing these styles of relationship. This is new because priests themselves--assigned by their bishops or provincials to a given parish--have often not expected much in the way of extensive relationships with their fellow priests. Some have achieved a kind of community in the rectory or friary, but this is not typical, and now most priests are finding themselves in parishes without any brother priest. The more relational or communal approach to ministry desired by these new ministers marks a change.

A Local Dimension

Third, for all our protests that ministry in the Catholic community is not congregational, the dynamics in place are leading to an increasingly **local** or congregational source and shaping of parish ministry. At the most extreme, pastors are often turning to parishioners to become part of the formal parish ministry. In acting this way, they are in fact imitating one aspect of how priests have been chosen. For the process of selecting, screening, and ordaining priests has always entailed a time of observing how well the candidates combined the necessary ecclesial and personal qualities for ministry. Pastors are inclined to do the same. While some hire ministers via diocesan and religious order "clearing-houses," in fact few dioceses or orders have clearing, screening or certifying procedures regarding these ministers, and pastors are as likely to "go with a known quantity." They look around at those they have seen, parishioners whom they have been able to observe volunteering in their parishes or lay people who have served in parish schools or other kinds of church ministry, where they have demonstrated the qualities required for good ministry. This trend would be more pronounced were it not for the fact that there are still so many sisters in parish ministry, but the tide has already turned. The sisters are already outnumbered by lay people and this will be increasingly true in the years ahead. Forty percent of the sisters in parish ministry are already over sixty years old, a quarter of them are over sixty-five, while less than ten percent of the lay people are over sixty.

But the local, and to some extent congregational trend in parish ministry is not simply a matter of numbers. It is also a matter of authority and responsibility for parish ministry, which have shifted appreciably away from the diocese and bishop and in the direction of the parish and pastor. Very few dioceses exercise much responsibility, to say nothing of authority, for determining just what ministry positions there will be (such as pastoral associate or pastoral minister) or who and with what qualifications will occupy these positions. Individual pastors, increasingly with their councils, are determining these matters, articulating positions, establishing criteria, and drawing up contracts with such ministers. Once the diocese and order were no longer the assured providers of ministers, they diminished their role in shaping the ministries. This may be just as well for the present, since parishes have needed considerable freedom for the emergence of new ministries and, in fact, pastors are remarkably pragmatic people who do what is necessary, rarely with any ideological intent.

Of course, the shift in this same localizing direction was made with permanent deacons. For although deacons are screened and ordained and assigned by diocesan leaders and bishops, still they typically require the approval of their pastors and typically serve in the parish where they have been parishioners.

With all the advantages and disadvantages that go with congregation-based ministry, which we will report, a significant part of parish ministry has become localized.

A Ministerial Dimension

The fourth development is an evolution of what it means to be ministerial. This is to say that ministry is its own species, a category of its own, and not best understood as a subset of some other functional category. Specifically, this is to say that ministry is not coterminous with being clerical, professional, vowed religious, or baptized. This needs some elaboration.

Formal ministry had become mostly clerical or religious, generally restricted to the clergy and those in vows. Ministry belonged to those who occupied these stable statuses in the church. This is no longer true.[7]

Recently, there has been a tendency to talk of ministry not as a status but as a "profession." This may not be apt. While there is no agreement among those who study occupations and professions about what actually constitutes a profession or a professional, the use of the category suggested formal theoretical education, training for performance, certification (by academic degree or some other institutional deputation), certain standards of performance, and an association or other structure that ensures communication among the members of the profession. For some, all these criteria can be reduced to one: control of some area of knowledge or service by a particular group.[8] In spite of the tendency in some areas of ministry to suggest that legitimacy depends on the appropriate academic degree (as in religious education or liturgy or music) or certification (as in youth ministry), the picture is more complex.

Finally, there has been a tendency to assert that all the baptized are ministers of the church. Even Pope John Paul II in *Familiaris consortio* has referred to the ministry of members of the family. To the extent that each shares responsibility for the community and mission of the church, this is true. But, parishes and dioceses are acknowledging that formal positions of ministry require varying degrees of understanding of the tradition of the church and the skills of community ministry. To minister is one thing, something all can do (just as we can all teach each other in some ways) but to **be** a minister (as to be a teacher) requires some formal knowledge and skills.

To bring all this together, the emphasis now in deputing people for ministry--by hiring or appointing them--more and more restores what was always the objective, namely a combination of ministerial and personal abilities. Pastors no longer automatically look for another priest or a religious (the status) to meet the needs of ministry, though surely many do. They do not always seek someone with a relevant degree (a professional) though they do appreciate good preparation. Often, pastors look for persons who have a record of working well with people, of personal religiosity, and, if not possessing the requisite knowledge and skills for the particular ministry, at least with the native ability and apparent readiness to acquire them. The shift from status to a combination of general relational abilities and specific ministerial competencies (perhaps in that order) is the point here.

This feature of contemporary ministry could be regarded as a corollary of the feminizing and localizing of ministry, for it entails some of the relational attributes often regarded as feminine qualities and the opportunity to observe one's performance which is easier when the person is already in the community. It also requires a personal perspective in another sense: relational qualities are not abstractions. They are ways that individuals relate to specific other individuals or groups and the pastors are looking for people who can relate to themselves and to the particular people of a particular parish, which again favors those who are near enough to be observed. Finally, pastors who are looking for this combination of traits in ministers do so because they have found the same combination to be valuable in their own lives and even find themselves challenged to the same ideals.

Another way to look at this trend is to locate the ideals for ministry somewhere on the spectrum between an overly reductionist popularizing of ministry and an inappropriately professional approach to ministry. The meaning of a reductionist

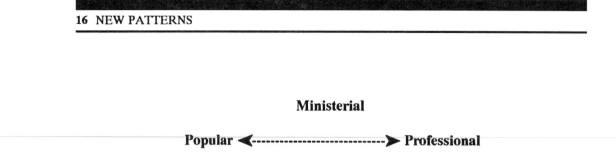

Ministerial

Popular ◀--------------------------▶ **Professional**

approach is evident enough: settling for ministerial leadership by people with so little formation in the tradition and theology of the church or contact with the universal church that they jeopardize that tradition and the links with the universal church.

The danger of professionalizing might be a little less evident, for much of the recent past has been a history of increasing the theological and pastoral formation of those who will exercise ministerial leadership. We are calling "professional" the overly narrow construing of ministry which is perhaps most evident in two expressions of parish life. One is the trend, which may be more bureaucratic than professional, in parishes toward establishing offices and office hours, secretaries, segmentation of roles, communication by paper and records, answering services and machines and all the devices that in themselves are valuable but which have the danger of making parishioners feel like "clients," who must seek services from the professional minister who in turn exercises more and more control over these services by introducing new prerequisites for receiving them.

The other example of "professional" tension in parish ministry involves especially the liturgists (and sometimes the musicians) in parish life. The schools of liturgy have done a remarkable job in preparing ministers with a much deeper and broader appreciation of liturgical theology, history, and symbolism than most priests have ever received. They have labored to set some standards for what was in danger of sinking into the worst of immanentism, sentimentalism, and trivializing of liturgical ministry, rites, and arts. Nonetheless, this has not been without a cost. Humor often reveals critical issues and it is no accident that a popular riddle of the day is the one that goes: "Q. What's the difference between a liturgist and a terrorist?...A. You can negotiate with a terrorist." The obvious meaning is that some liturgists are intractable in their insistence on certain professional standards or practices in liturgy. In the past, something of this tension arose when religious education seemed to be emerging as a professional specialty. Stories circulated about priests who were suddenly told not to interfere in the religious education program because they were not expert in that area and, conversely, of priests who showed no respect for those who had done studies in religious education. So today tensions--which can be good tensions--exist between the demands of liturgists and what are seen by pastors, other ministers, or parishioners to be other important considerations.

There is one other way in which ministry is distinct from a profession, though we are on dangerous ground here. Ministry requires that the minister become what s/he is trying to help others become. We do not want to fall into the heresy that ministry depends entirely on the holiness of the minister. It does not. Nor do we want to claim that parishioners themselves cannot accept ministry from any but the holy, any but an elite. There is no evidence of this and plenty of evidence to the contrary. In fact, in the mode of the twelve-step programs or even of Damien's "we lepers" admission, it is often what Henri Nouwen has called the "wounded healer" who can minister best, not by nursing the woundedness but by sharing the pursuit of healing. What it means to be holy is seen to embrace more human qualities than might once have been involved. It is not only one's relationship with God, but also one's efforts at healthy relationships with oneself (one's physical and emotional health) and with others, as well as one's stance regarding culture that affect one's ability to minister. This is not true as much of other occupations or professions--the doctor's health habits are not the patient's business (though in the case of AIDS this has become a factor in doctor-patient relationships); the lawyer's own legal situation is not the client's concern.

In the context of this discussion, we want to suggest that formal parish ministry is not a profession. It shares many of the qualities we assign to or expect from professions--the need for a grounding in theory (theology), its own special language and terms, the ability to apply one's learning to particular situations, the value of some form of accreditation, the ethics of behavior--but in two critical ways it is distinct from a profession. Parish ministry is not trying to control access to its primary resources--the grace of relationship with God and with one another or the creative and redemptive power of the Spirit--nor even of the right to exercise ministry (which John Paul II has found in every family member). Neither can it see or treat parishioners as clients. Rather, ministry is a category of its own. This is becoming clear in the evolution of ministry.

Some Other Trends: Personnel Systems, Missing Minorities

There are other aspects of the present revolution that require attention. Some of these might be captured under the heading of "**personnel issues**." Again, the church is beneficiary to developments in other parts of the culture. The more complex the ministry, the more attentive the pastors have to be to good procedures for hiring, delegation of responsibility, supervision, compensation including benefits, termination of employment, and working conditions. Justice and legality as well as ethics and respect for people's dignity call for much more attentiveness to these matters. In addition, financial compensation for ministry is an increasingly important issue not only for lay persons but also for religious in parish ministry. It is the single most difficult aspect of the working conditions in parish ministry.[9]   In fact, there is evidence that, if we do not do better in the amount we pay people, many will not be able to continue in ministry especially if a reversal of the present recession will increase the number of other opportunities for employment available.

Secondly, what has already been noted by many is further confirmed by our study: there is a drastic problem of the **very few Hispanic and African-American ministers**. Fewer than five percent of the parish ministers are people of color. Even among the lay ministers we are studying, where leadership does not call for ordination--whatever obstacles exist in these communities regarding the present discipline of ordination--we have not been able to develop much indigenous church leadership among the African-American and Hispanic communities.[10] The diaconate still seems to be the most successful way in which African-American and Hispanic Catholics have been brought into pastoral leadership positions.[11] More strenuous and creative efforts are necessary to increase African-American and Hispanic leadership for their own communities and for the whole church.

State of the Development

In light of all these dramatic developments, how goes this revolution? Quite well indeed. By whatever measure we could devise, these new ministers are doing very well. We examined the ministers' effectiveness regarding a host of parish ministries, their satisfaction with their work, their relationships with parishioners and pastors, their working conditions, and their sense of accomplishment. In every respect, all involved provide an extraordinarily positive report. These parish ministers improve the quality and outreach of most parish ministries. The great majority have clear responsibilities and adequate authority, are in situations where staff communication, cooperation, and mutual support are well-organized, enjoy adequate working conditions, and derive considerable satisfaction from their ministry. Obviously, the situation is far from perfect. We will be pointing to matters that need various levels of attention if the church is to build a sound ministerial future on what the past twenty-five years have produced. Yet, the overwhelming message that comes through this study is that dedicated people have figured out how to exercise and share ministry with realistic adjustments to current and sometimes inevitable constraints.[12]

II: Where Are the Parish Ministers?

L ay parish ministry has not spread evenly across the country, from diocese to diocese, or parish to parish, as might be expected. Extrapolating from our survey, slightly more than half the parishes of the country (54 percent) have employed religious and laity in at least part-time (twenty hours or more) parish ministry positions. Not surprisingly, the parishes most likely to hire lay parish ministers tend to be the larger parishes and the parishes with larger incomes.

These parishes are likely to be found in the suburbs and the middle-class sections of cities. At the other end of the spectrum are the inner city parishes and those in rural/farm and resort areas, which are smaller, have smaller incomes, and hire fewer parish personnel. Thus, 65 percent of what we have grouped together as "small parishes" have **no** lay parish ministers, while 35 percent of the middle-size parishes have not hired lay ministers, and 18 percent of the large parishes have not

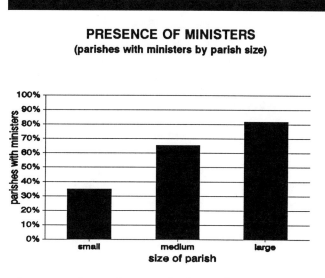

PRESENCE OF MINISTERS
(parishes with ministers by parish size)

hired them.* The relationships become clear when we look at the percentage of parishes in each type of area that has hired parish ministers (see table on the next page).

But size and income are not everything; if they were, there would be a perfect correlation (in statistical terms =1.00) between those factors and the presence and number of lay ministers on staff. But this is not true. In fact, the correlation of the total number of hired staff with **parish size** (or number of registered parishioners) is .3054. In statistical terms, this means that parish size explains less than 10 percent

* Small=fewer than 1000 registered parishioners; middle size=1001 to 2500; large=more than 2500.

of the variation in numbers of staff. The correlation of total number of hired staff to parish **income** is even smaller, .2300, accounting for about 5 percent of the variation.

What accounts for a parish's hiring staff is actually a combination of factors. The pastor is more likely to hire religious and laity for parish ministry, if the parish is large and has enough money. Also, the relative wealth of the parishioners in these large parishes has a positive effect on whether any parish ministers are hired and how many are hired. Note that **parish** income makes more of a difference than parishioners' own income, that is, if pastors we surveyed have been good judges in estimating the income levels of their parishioners.

Curiously, it is not the number of organized ministries nor the degree to which the parish style is an organized one that disposes the pastor to hire staff. *From our site visits, we draw a different inference. Some pastors, influenced perhaps by their having been associates in parishes with staffs, or by their having worked in schools, offices, or agencies where there were staff members with various specialties, seem "staff-oriented," where other pastors facing similar pastoral demands seem less inclined to put money into staffs.[13]*

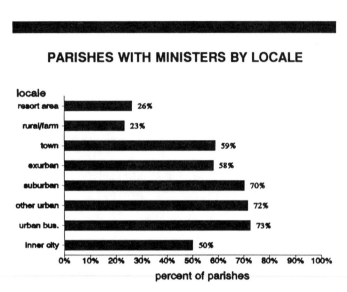

PARISHES WITH MINISTERS BY LOCALE

locale
resort area	26%
rural/farm	23%
town	59%
exurban	58%
suburban	70%
other urban	72%
urban bus.	73%
inner city	50%

0% 10% 20% 30% 40% 50% 60% 70% 80% 90% 100%
percent of parishes

**RELIGIOUS EDUCATORS IN PARISHES
WITH AND WITHOUT SCHOOLS**
(percent)

PARISHES	With School	No School
With Religious Educator	51.4	31.1
Without Religious Educator	48.6	68.9
TOTAL	100.0	100.0

For the majority of parishes, especially the large ones, the presence of a school does not significantly determine whether or not a parish hires lay parish ministers. Although, it has often been averred that the money going into a school is taken away from the rest of the parish, where it might serve a larger portion of the parish, in fact the more money a parish is putting into a school from the general parish income (over and above any tuition income), the more likely it is that the parish is also putting money into pastoral staff. The much stated objection that school support robs money from religious education for the rest of the parish is not accurate: again the more parishes spend on a school, the more likely they are to have staff for religious education.

Smaller and poorer parishes, however, are somewhat less able to hire staff and here the school does make a difference: the smaller inner city and other parishes that do have schools are less likely to be able to have other pastoral staffs--they more often have to make a choice between school support and other pastoral staff. (It may also be true that the school personnel in inner city parishes are somewhat more ready to extend their ministry beyond the school; this is an impression we have from our work with parish life, but we cannot state this categorically.) Among the small parishes, the absence of lay ministers is associated with the poverty of the parish, the poverty of the people, and the presence of a school. Again, just as all large parishes with ample income do not turn that income into staff salaries, so this does not mean that all small, poor parishes do without other parish staff. It does mean, however, that they are likely to go without because of their poverty or their choice of running a school.

Do lay ministers substitute for priests? Obviously, the dramatic growth of these ministries has occurred at the time when the number of priests in parish ministry have been declining. Whereas, just ten year ago (according to the Notre Dame Study), half the parishes in the United States had only one priest, now almost two-thirds do. In that gross sense, clearly the lay/religious parish ministers are compensating for the lack of priests, though they, of course, do more than that. Furthermore, it was specialization as much as substitution that led to the hiring of these parish ministers as is evident from the fact that the first, major innovation in parish ministry, namely the hiring of religious education coordinators, began before the decline in numbers of priests set in.

NUMBER OF PRIESTS PER PARISH

Number of Priests	Number of Parishes	Percent of Parishes
0	9	0.8
1	737	63.3
2	258	22.2
3	102	8.8
4	43	3.7
5	12	1.0
6	3	0.3

Do we, however, find that the fewer the numbers of priests available, the greater number of lay ministers hired? In a sense yes, but only when we look at the numbers of priests relative to the sizes of parishes. For, in fact, the more priests there are in parishes, the more these parishes also have lay/religious parish ministers. For the larger parishes have more priests, but also more activities, and more demands than the priests can handle, and more resources for hiring lay ministers. Whether or not the pastor recognizes the value of having the variety of competencies and genders that lay and religious ministers bring, he will often need the extra help for meeting the demands of ministry. The large table detailing the priest and other parish staff ratios by the regions of the country shows that even this is not a uniform picture, however.

REGIONAL DIFFERENCES IN PASTORAL STAFFING
(averages)

Region	States Encompassed by Region	Priests Per Parish	Pastoral Ministers Per Parish	Total Pastoral Staff Per Parish	Mass Attenders Per Priest	Mass Attenders Per Pastoral Staff Member
1	CT ME MA NH RI VT	1.63	0.98	2.61	775	525
2	NY	2.04	1.30	3.34	689	419
3	NJ PA	1.57	0.91	2.48	902	712
4	DE DC FL GA MD NC SC VA WV	1.87	1.20	3.07	680	496
5	AL KY LA MS TN	1.45	0.69	2.14	571	448
6	OH MI	1.38	1.35	2.73	938	530
7	IL IN WISC	1.32	0.69	2.01	481	340
8	MN ND SD	1.24	1.12	2.36	681	394
9	IA KS MO NE	1.25	0.77	2.01	646	433
10	AR OK TX	1.04	1.12	2.15	616	379
11	CA HW NV	2.20	1.69	3.89	766	472
12	AK ID MT OR WA	1.14	1.33	2.45	567	267
13	AZ CO NM UT WY	1.38	1.03	2.42	743	506

The table above gives a picture of some regional variations in parish staffing. The average number of priests per parish is highest in the western region of California, Hawaii, and Nevada with 2.2 per parish and in the New York State diocese with 2.04 per parish. The opposite end of the continuum is represented by the southwest region that takes in Arizona, Oklahoma, and Texas with 1.04 priests per parish and the northwest region (Alaska, Idaho, Montana, Oregon, and Washington) with 1.14 priests per parish. Two of the three regions that have added the largest numbers of lay and religious parish ministers to their staffs are those with the most priests--California, Hawaii, Nevada and New York State--as well as the region that includes Ohio and Michigan. The regions with the least number of parish ministers per parish are the southern region (Region 5) that includes Alabama, Kentucky, Louisiana, Mississippi, and Tennessee and the midwest region that embrces Iowa, Kansas, Missouri, and Nebraska. To some extent, these regional variations are really once again size variations, that is, the priests and parish ministers are needed to staff large parishes.

When we look at the regions in terms of how much the addition of lay ministers helps to reduce the number of parishioners in relation to any staff member, priest or lay, measured in terms of Mass attenders per staff member, the regions with the most pronounced changes are: Regions 6 (Ohio, Michigan), 12 (Alaska, Idaho, Montana, Oregon, and Washington), and 8 (Minnesota, North Dakota, South Dakota), and 2 (New York State). Those where the relatively few lay ministers have least affected the parishioner-staff ratio are the southern Region 5 and Region 7 (Illinois, Indiana, Wisconsin) which regions were already among those best staffed, that is, with the smallest number of parishioners per priest. In other words, the addition of lay ministers in a very general way has obviously been used to improve the parishioner-staff ratio, but in varying degrees throughout the dioceses and regions of the country. Before discussing this, we need to say a word about nomenclature. The terms used for parish positions vary and the same term can have quite different meanings as we shall see in the next section. At this point it is enough for us to say something about the positions that involve a variety of responsibilities in parish life. The terms used here most often are "pastoral associate" (as distinct from the commonly used "associate pastor" for an ordained curate) and "pastoral minister." We will use the term "**general** pastoral minister" to refer to both these categories, while we will use the term "pastoral minister" or "parish minister" as a term for all these religious and lay people who are in all the non-school, pastoral staff positions in parishes. (In some few instances, we will still want to speak specifically about those who are "pastoral associates" because this title usually represents the fullest equivalent to an ordained parish minister.)

Smaller and poorer parishes are somewhat more likely to hire general pastoral ministers--the new pastoral associates or pastoral ministers--than ministers for a particular ministry such as religious education or youth ministry. Small parishes are two-thirds as likely as medium size parishes to have pastoral associates and their comparison with large parishes is about the same, but they are only a third as likely as medium size parishes and even less than large parishes to have religious educators. They are even less likely, as compared with medium size and large parishes, to have youth ministers or liturgists.

**MINISTRY POSITIONS BY LOCALE:
PRESENCE OF RELIGIOUS EDUCATORS
AND GENERAL PARISH MINISTERS**
(percent)

LOCALE	With Any Parish Minister on Staff (1)	With Religious Educator on Staff (2)	With General Pastoral Minister on Staff (3)
Inner City	54	33	31
Business	70	57	29
Other Urban	74	63	30
Suburban	73	71	25
Exurban	65	65	12
Small Town	60	61	21
Rural/Farm	21	22	9
Resort	30	17	9

To add social condition to size, more than half of all the inner city parish ministers are general pastoral ministers, while general pastoral ministers account for only little more than a quarter of all the pastoral ministers. (Compare columns 1 and 3.) Similarly, general pastoral ministers account for a higher percentage of all the parish ministers in rural/farm parishes (as well as in business parishes which tend to have little staff, though it is surprising that more than half of these parishes with staffs have directors of religious education as well). But this kind of variation seems regional as well. To hire a person specifically as a "pastoral associate" reflects a later stage of lay ministry than does the position of director of religious education and this position more nearly approximates the roles of ordained associate. Even among the larger parishes, the persons in this role constitute a smaller portion of all the staff members in the northeast of the country than in other areas.

Obviously enough, the other specialized ministries are more likely to be found in larger parishes, especially where the parish can hire more than one staff member, though the pattern is a little more nuanced than that. The liturgists are more likely to be found in the large urban and suburban parishes. The youth ministers are even more likely to be in the suburban/exurban areas where the parishes are larger. The musicians, however, while they are found in almost half the suburban parishes are even more likely to be found in the urban middle class and business parishes and even four of ten inner city parishes have hired musicians at least on a part-time basis.

We should not go any further regarding paid staff without acknowledging that some people who work extensively in parish ministry do so on a volunteer basis. The Notre Dame Study had found that among those named as volunteer leaders of various parish ministries, 30 percent averaged twenty-five hours a month or more doing parish work, many of these devoting "almost all their discretionary time to parish activities."[14] In fact, one diocese reports that while there are 109 full-time paid lay persons in the parishes of its rural deaneries, there are also 98 full-time

unpaid lay persons on staffs; the number of unpaid lay persons in its urban deaneries is only 30 (as compared with 220 paid full-time persons).

Does hiring paid staff then discourage what in one kind of language is called volunteerism but in more theological terms might be called the stewardship responsibilities of the members of the parish community? In other words, can we detect less volunteering in parishes with paid staffs or do these new parish ministers actually make it possible for more parishioners to be involved. We cannot quantify the effects of lay and religious parish ministers on parishioner volunteering, in the usual meaning of that term. We did get abundant reports from the surveys that these ministers make a difference in involving people in parish life, some segments of parish membership more than others. *Our site visits also elicited abundant testimony from both the parish ministers themselves and the pastors and parishioners that the involvement of the parishioners was a goal and an accomplishment of these ministers. As a matter of fact, for the most part, the lay ministers put a premium on engaging parishioners in ministry and are seen by the pastor and parishioners as doing this. In some instances, this responsibility is quite pronounced. In one parish with a decidedly "charismatic" style of leadership and ministry, the paid staff largely provides organization and coordination while parishioner groups take responsibility for all the ministries; in another parish a sister is the coordinator of thirty-eight ministry groups of parishioners; in a third, there is a "pastoral associate for planning" who serves as an administrator and as a coordinator or administrative assistant for ministries.* It is also worth noting that the majority of those in paid positions (58 percent) indicate that part of their responsibility is ministry training of the parishioners and almost three-quarters of the general pastoral ministers equip parishioners in this way for more involvement in parish ministry. To be sure, there are some parishes where it is evident that the paid staff directly provides the ministry and some of the ministers themselves acknowledged to us that they do not do as well as they should in engaging parishioners and maintaining the stance that responsibility for the life and mission of the parish remain primarily with parishioners themselves.

III: Profile, Preparation, and Entry into the Parish

We are describing a rather new phenomenon in the church, the transformation of parish ministry from an almost totally clerical ministry to one shared with lay persons and religious. We do not know how long individual parishes have had various ministry positions open to lay persons and religious, but we can report that more than half (59 percent) of all these ministers have been in their present positions five years or less. In the older positions--religious education and music--a quarter of the ministers have served ten years or more, while fewer than a fifth of the general pastoral ministers or other minsters have been in their present position that long. The youth ministers face special obstacles to longevity, which we will discuss below, but for the present we can note that not one in twenty of them has been in the position as long as ten years. In every category of ministry (associates, religious education, liturgy, etc.), the largest group of the ministers have been in their positions two to three years. Most do intend to stay: half or more for the foreseeable future. Only about one in ten was getting ready to leave their positions.[15]

How have these ministries developed? What kind of people have been looking to get into these ministries and what have pastors been looking for? Before elaborating on these questions, some basic elements of the demographic profile of these ministers will be useful.[16]

Profile of the Ministers

Slightly more than half of these parish ministers are lay (58 percent) and the rest are religious (42 percent) of whom the vast majority are sisters--only seven tenths of one percent are brothers. It is worth noting that three percent are former religious and six-tenths of a percent or six persons in our sample are inactive priests (we have counted both these groups among the laity in the rest of this report). We found that pastors are almost evenly divided on whether they prefer lay persons or religious for these positions, with slightly more (52 percent) preferring a lay person which usually means a lay woman.

The site visits helped us to understand that the motives related to either preference vary. Some of those who prefer sisters think that they bring a richer background in church ministry and the witness value of religious life to the ministry; some find the sisters less expensive to hire; some simply have had good experiences with sisters. Among those who prefer lay women, some think that their lay experience is helpful to the ministry, some that the lay persons bring fewer needs to their work in the parish, some that the lay people have a more philosophical attitude regarding the role of women in the church.[17]

Eighty-five percent of the new parish ministers are women, 15 percent men. It is especially in youth ministry (41 percent) and music ministry (52 percent) that the men are to be found --they account for about half of the full-timers in each of these. Of the lay persons, almost two-thirds are married while a quarter have never been married; four percent are widowed and nine percent are separated or divorced. The ratio of married to single is the same among full-time and part-time lay ministers.

Given the advancing age of sisters in the country and the fact that the sisters in parish ministry have usually come from other ministries, it is not surprising, to find, as we have indicated, that about forty percent of the sisters are over sixty and a quarter of them are even over sixty-five. Parishes share the forecast of other ministries that the present dependence on women religious will progressively diminish. Only eight percent of the lay ministers are over sixty--the vast majority are in their mid-thirties to mid-fifties--except when it comes to the youth ministers, who are appreciably younger, as are those in music ministry. We will look at each of the ministries further on.

It is regrettable that only about five percent are other than white: almost four percent are Hispanic--about twice as prevalent among the lay as religious--and a little less than one percent are African-American, most of whom are lay.[18] Another half of a percent are Asian or Native American.

PROFILE OF PASTORAL MINISTERS

CATEGORY	Total #	%
Religious	404	41.5
397 Sisters		
7 Brothers		
Lay	570	58.5
535 Lay		
29 Former Religious		
6 Inactive Priests		
Total	974	100.0

CATEGORY	Totals #	%
Men	142	14.6
135 Lay		
7 Religious		
Women	832	85.4
435 Lay		
397 Religious		
Total	974	100.0

AGES OF LAITY AND RELIGIOUS

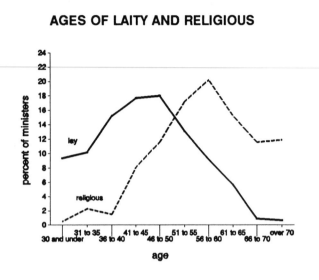

The parish ministers are a well-educated group. Half have master's degrees or even more education and another quarter have completed college, some of whom have done further graduate work. Only a fifth have less education than that. The religious are about twice as well-educated as the lay persons: 80 percent of them have a master's degree or better and all but four percent have completed college. Of the lay persons, three out of ten have not completed college and only a third have master's degrees or further education. The differences become even more pronounced when we look at the lay persons who are working part-time, for these have somewhat less education. We will discuss education in more detail later in this chapter.

We wondered how often lay persons coming into church ministry had undergone what has often been called a "conversion experience" in the past, perhaps through contact with one of the more expressive or ecstatic movements in the church or even in a missionary experience that can inspire intense commitment.[19] But we were interested not just in those experiences but in various experiences that fostered deeper faith commitment. We inquired about the movement background of the lay ministers in our interviews and through the surveys by asking about prior "movement" experience. Some of the ministers did talk about having had the emotionally powerful

PARTICIPATION IN GROUPS OR MOVEMENTS
(percent that led or took part)

Marriage Encounter	21.5
Charismatic Renewal	25.2
Cursillo	22.7
Christian Family Movement	5.1
Search, TEC, Antioch	13.1
RENEW	25.8
Other	12.4

experience of some movement in their background (one who had been in the Jesuit Volunteer Corp and then went to law school, but wanted to work in the church and does so in a social ministry, advocacy position).

The data in the table on page 28 do not indicate separate individuals; many could well have been involved in more than one such group. Nonetheless, many have had such a group experience. Of course, these could have participated in any of these groups since they became ministers and thus these cannot be considered as necessarily a route to parish ministry. But whether an earlier or later experience, they do represent a considerable relationship between groups devoted to more personal engagement in faith and church and participation in the ministry of the church.[20]

Other qualities of these new ministers and aspects of their entry into their present parish position bear consideration. First, apart from teaching, many of these ministers have worked in other parishes. For four out of ten of the religious, this is not their first parish ministry experience and a quarter of the lay persons have also worked in other parishes. Why did they leave their previous position--whether it was in teaching or some other form of parish ministry? About 40 percent were looking for something "more"--more money (5 percent), more responsibility (6 percent), the opportunity to work with adults (4 percent), or simply a change from what they were doing (26 percent). About 17 percent we might attribute to something negative about the previous position: conflict or a change of pastor, and almost another 7 percent report that their prior position had been discontinued.

Some saw the new position as meeting more of their concerns regarding the mission of the church and for about seven percent (mostly lay persons of course) family relocation necessitated leaving the previous position. A quarter had a complex of reasons.

The vast majority of the lay and religious parish ministers come from at least moderately religious families themselves; two-thirds from families they regard as having been very religious. The ministers themselves are obviously quite religious and have become more so in recent years, whether as a direct result of their ministry in the church or for other reasons--more general trends in the church toward more concern for spirituality or even the simple fact that they are older now--we cannot say. But while 70 percent (77 percent of the religious, 66 percent of the lay people) report having felt quite close (1-2 on a scale of five) to **God** five years ago, nine out of ten feel that way now (93 percent of the religious, 87 percent of the laity). (In this respect, the pastors' reports of their own relationships to God are quite the same as the lay persons, which is to say not quite as intense as that of the religious.) The ministers' relationship to the **church** reflects the same trend if not quite the same strength of relationship. We did not define "church" but the question was located between one about "God" and another about their "parish" and so probably was inferred to mean the universal church. More than seven out of ten parish ministers feel quite close to the church and somewhat fewer (64 percent) felt this way five years ago. Their feelings about their **parish** lie between the two, but have shown almost as much improvement as their relationship with God: from two-thirds feeling quite close to almost eight-tenths feeling that way. Again, the feelings of religious are slightly stronger. It should be a matter of satisfaction that the more people minister in the parish the closer they come to feel to God, the church, and the parish. It should also be a matter of concern, we suspect, that a tenth do not feel so close to God and a fifth to a quarter or more do not feel close to either their parish or the church. It is interesting to note that the lay people who are part-time feel somewhat closer to the church and the parish than the full-timers.

RELATIONSHIPS TO GOD, CHURCH AND PARISH AMONG PARISH MINISTERS
(percent)

CATEGORY	Total Ministers	Lay	Religious	Pastors
Relationship to God				
Close now	89.4	86.7	93.2	85.7
Close five years ago	70.4	65.8	76.8	68.8
Relationship to Church				
Close now	71.7	71.2	72.4	73.0
Close five years ago	63.9	60.7	68.3	75.8
Relationship to Parish				
Close now	78.3	72.4	81.3	N/A
Close five years ago	65.6	68.3	70.2	N/A

The spiritual practices of parish ministers, as reflected in the table on the following page, is quite strong: seven out of ten take part in the Eucharist daily or, at least, more often than weekly (almost all of the religious and half of the lay persons). Seven of ten describe their prayer life as "regular" (vs. "erratic" or "seldom apart from the prayer activities of my ministry") as compared with fewer than six out of ten of the pastors claiming this (and almost one-tenth of the pastors indicating that they pray little outside of the prayers of their ministry). The strong pattern of spiritual practices, particularly among the religious, is both a great contribution to the parishes where they minister and an indication of the expectations they bring to their work with pastors and other ministers.

SPIRITUAL PRACTICES OF PARISH MINISTERS
(percent)

CATEGORY	Lay	Religious	Pastors
Mass Attendance			
Daily or several times per week	51.7	94.3	N/A
Weekly	43.6	5.5	N/A
Several times per month	2.6	0.0	N/A
Monthly or less	2.2	0.3	N/A
Prayer Life			
Regular	61.2	84.4	57.1
Erratic	35.1	13.3	32.5
Seldom apart from ministry	3.8	2.3	9.0
Types of Prayer Practiced			
Liturgy of hours	27.1	83.4	80.1
Meditation	63.7	90.2	68.6
Scripture reading	73.2	89.2	70.0
Devotions	40.6	60.6	64.0
Other	30.0	36.0	23.0

Education and Training for Ministry

Preparation for parish ministry takes many forms: formal education in pertinent subjects, spiritual formation, training in the skills needed for the role, and, we might add, socialization into the culture of the church. In many or most of these respects, the parish ministers are quite well prepared indeed. Of course, almost half of them are religious who have been in church ministry for some time and have extensive preparation for and experience in ministry. For this reason, in reporting the preparation of these parish ministers, we will of course have to distinguish repeatedly between the religious and the laity.[21]

EDUCATIONAL BACKGROUND: LAY VS. RELIGIOUS
(percent)

LEVEL OF EDUCATION	Lay	Religious
High school or less	7.9	1.2
Some college or other post high school	23.3	2.9
College graduate	18.9	7.2
Some graduate work	16.6	8.2
Master's degree	30.0	76.9
M.Div.	1.4	1.7
D.Min.	0.5	0.2
Doctorate	1.4	1.5

Eighty percent of all these parish ministers have at least a college education and the vast majority of these (52.7 percent of the total) have a master's degree or better. This is a very well-educated population.

Yet we would be remiss were we not to note: (1) how much more educated the religious are; (2) that this very well-educated resource of religious in pastoral ministry will surely diminish considerably in coming years; and (3) that the educational profile of parish ministers will probably more resemble that of the laity at present unless future parish lay ministers are better educated. A look at the lay ministers by age indicates that the younger are indeed more educated. But let us look further at education and training before making comments.

Almost 10 percent of the total had eight years of Catholic schooling, another 30 percent had between nine and twelve years, a quarter had thirteen to sixteen years of Catholic education, and another 16 percent had even more. The religious have had more Catholic schooling than the lay ministers have.

MAJOR FIELDS OF STUDY OF PARISH MINISTERS
(percent)

FIELD OF STUDY	Highest Degree	Second Equivalent Level Degree
Theology	9.1	2.6
Religious Education	12.9	4.6
Pastoral Ministry	4.9	2.2
Liturgy	1.0	0.8
Combination (pastoral)	3.8	0.8
Non-pastoral combination	0.8	1.5
Music	7.0	1.3
Education	23.0	6.2
Counselling/Psychology	3.5	1.8
Social Work	1.4	0.3
Liberal Arts	5.9	1.4
Social Science	1.0	0.8
Business	3.9	0.5
Administration	3.0	1.9
Other	9.7	8.0
None	9.2	65.0

What was the content of this education and how well does it relate to their work as pastoral ministers? The table to the left indicates the fields of the highest degree or degrees for each minister.

Once we look into the fields of education, we might conclude that there is not a great deal of formal education in the more directly religious fields: theology, religious education, pastoral ministry, and liturgy. At this point we might look at how well prepared the pastoral ministers themselves think they are in the fields related to their work.

We asked the pastoral ministers (and the pastors) about ten subject areas which might be related to the pastoral ministers' ministries. The following table indicates whether parish ministers think their work requires knowledge in each area and how well prepared they feel and the pastors' views of how well prepared the parish ministers are.

Clearly, the pastoral ministers feel better prepared in the theological areas than their formal education might suggest. And the pastors tend to endorse their view. There is evidently room for further education in these areas as the pastoral ministers themselves acknowledge.

MINISTERS' WORK AND PREPARATION FOR IT:
PARISH MINISTERS' AND PASTORS' VIEWS
(percent)

SUBJECT	"Important to Work"	"Adequately Prepared?"	
	Ministers' View	Ministers' View	Pastors' View
Scripture	88.6	66.4	64.1
Doctrine	79.3	63.4	62.9
Moral Theology	74.9	52.9	54.1
Liturgy	78.7	62.6	66.7
Spirituality	87.5	70.8	65.5
Family Life	70.9*	48.6	65.1
Social Services	50.3*	31.6	54.3
Justice Concerns	62.0	38.7	43.1
Youth Development	59.9	45.9	55.5
Elderly Concerns	42.0	31.2	62.9

*   In almost all categories, especially those marked with an asterisk, the pastors (speaking about all the lay ministers they have) are far more likely to think that this is involved in the lay ministers' work.

Obviously, those involved in religious education, preaching, or other forms of teaching have greater need for a good theological formation. Also, the great number of ministers who are involved in some form of Bible study, reflection or prayer group need to be well-versed in the Scriptures if they are to be good guides. Furthermore, the significant number of pastoral ministers who are involved in liturgy preparation and leadership far exceeds those with theological or liturgical education. [22]

In addition to these degree programs, we asked about non-degree programs the parish ministers might have taken part in. (See the table on the next page.)   The

NON-DEGREE TRAINING OF PARISH MINISTERS
(percent)

FIELD OF STUDY	One Training Program	Second Training Program
Theology	9.9	6.0
Religious Education	28.1	12.9
Pastoral Ministry	16.0	9.8
Liturgy	3.0	5.7
Music	4.4	2.6
Education	3.0	2.0
Counselling/Psychology	2.4	3.6
Social Work	1.0	1.0
Combination (pastoral)	3.2	2.1
Administration	1.8	2.3
Business	0.3	0.9
Other	7.2	5.4
None	19.7	45.4

vast majority (87.3 percent) have experienced programs of this kind, half of which (52 percent) were sponsored by the dioceses, while other sponsors in order of frequency were universities (16 percent), professional organizations (13 percent), parishes alone or in cooperation with the diocese (7 percent), and seminaries (3 percent). Not surprisingly, the content of these primarily church sponsored programs was more directly church related. Almost 80 percent of all the parish ministers had been in one of these programs and for 60 percent of these, the program led to some form of certification. About half of the ministers took part in a second such program which led to certification for 41.5 percent of them.

To complete this picture of education and training, we provided the ministers with a list of pastoral skills and asked them to indicate whether these skills were part of their work and whether their training adequately prepared them in these areas. Our list of skills and our findings are summarized in the table on the following page.

We will discuss in Chapter 8 how well parish ministers think they perform these skills, whatever the adequacy of their preparation. For the present, it is worth noting those where they especially feel inadequately prepared. Some items are admittedly rather vague, but they do capture the kinds of abilities called for in parish life. "Motivating people to become involved," for example, is not easily translated into a training program, but there is something of what might be called marketing here--the presentation of concerns in such a way as to appeal to people's values and interests-- and what has come to be called "enablement"--encouraging people to take some action and giving them the means to feel confident in doing so. Similarly, "hospitality" is obviously a broad term but denotes the attempt to be welcoming, inviting, a good host to people. Both suggest a kind of strategic thinking, the kind of thinking urged in the NCCB document on "family perspective." In that document parish staffs are encouraged to learn about the actual nature and concerns of families within their parishes and so to adapt existing parish activities (from Mass times to educational programs) to, and design new programs for, the specific needs of the various groups.

MINISTRY ACTIVITIES OF PARISH MINISTERS
(percent in order of frequency)

ACTIVITIES	Part of My Work	Adequately Prepared
Communicating one-on-one	87.4	77.0
Planning	84.5	72.9
Building community	80.0	68.1
Organizing projects	79.4	66.0
Collaborating	79.1	65.4
Motivating involvment	78.1	53.0
Communicating to public groups	76.9	63.6
Teaching (content)	74.9	68.0
Supervising others	71.4	55.4
Training (skills)	70.4	60.0
Leading/co-leading prayer	70.1	59.1
Hospitality	70.0	61.7
Administrating	68.8	56.0
Managing conflict	63.3	37.2
Preparing liturgies	58.6	47.4
Counselling	45.1	29.9
Visiting (i.e., homes, hospitals)	41.6	35.4
Spiritual directing	33.5	23.5
Performing (musically)	23.7	20.6
Preaching	14.6	13.1

A significant portion of the parish ministers feel ill prepared to supervise and train others for the ministerial work of the parish. Yet, the majority are called upon to do some training and supervision. We did not ask the pastors or other ordained ministers how well prepared they feel for these same works, but we dare say they would feel similarly ill-prepared. For supervision and training are activities or abilities whose importance we are only beginning to appreciate and for which some training programs are already available.

In general, the parish ministers feel slightly better prepared for certain "skills" than in the "content" areas of theology and ministry. But, more importantly, the lists give us an indication of the areas involved in pastoral ministry from the point of view of the ministers themselves. This can serve as a guide for ministry education and training programs. Furthermore, continuing education and training programs might best address those areas where the parish ministers feel less well prepared or where their prior education and training does not seem adequate to the tasks they are called upon to perform (e.g., liturgy preparation). Nonetheless, the parish ministers do have extensive education and training and this is a real contribution to parish ministry.

Hiring Approaches

Combining these features of parish ministers with consideration of how they got into the various ministries, let us look at the picture that emerges from our site visits and our surveys. First, we will look at the patterns of hiring, especially of lay persons, then at the religious.

Approaches to hiring parish ministers vary considerably among the parishes. Some pastors adopt a rather "professional" approach, such as one large southwest parish with seventeen people on staff, including a professionally trained liturgy director who enjoys a national reputation, a social ministry director who has social service training, a pastoral associate who came to the parish with both a master's degree in theology and experience as a pastoral associate in other parishes. Other pastors place a higher premium on their own prior personal experience with the individual, either as a minister in another parish (though only 3 percent of the lay ministers and almost 1

**HOW PASTORS RECRUIT PARISH STAFF:
THOSE WITH PAID PASTORAL MINISTERS ONLY**
(percent)

Recruit from people you know	81.7
Ads in parish bulletin(s)	37.7
Diocesan recruiting/clearing house	38.2
Ads in diocesan or other local paper	20.2
Ads in national papers, publications	10.4
Contact with religious orders	36.1
Contact colleges, universities, etc.	11.8
Other	3.5

percent of the religious have been with the pastor in a previous parish) or as a parishioner who has been active in the parish on a volunteer basis. The pastors in our study overwhelmingly (82 percent) reported looking first among people they knew when they needed a new staff member. In a few instances, a parishioner has even suggested establishing a particular ministry and the pastor has agreed.

Obviously, the extent to which a parish and pastor adopt a "professional" approach or a "popular" one will depend in part on the size and income of the parish, as we have noted. Some have considerable resources because of the size and income level of the parish and can afford "top dollar" in hiring ministers. Others are quite small, have scarce resources, and must depend largely on parishioners for any ministry to be done.

Many of the lay women seem to come from among the parishioners, volunteering and then being invited by the pastor to take a position. In fact, from the surveys, the vast majority of lay persons had been active as volunteers (about nine out of ten) before being hired and almost half the lay persons (43 percent of those employed full-time and slightly more of the part-timers) indicated that the pastor's personal invitation was one of their reasons for entering church ministry. At the same time more than two-thirds of these lay persons have earlier employment experience, about half of them (52 percent) in profit-making corporations and half (48 percent) in non-profit organizations, and more than half (about 70 percent) of these served in some professional capacity, as distinct from a support-staff position.

We asked these ministers what had motivated them to enter church ministry. As might be expected, the answers of the religious pointed to the special features of religious community as well as to the challenges of ministry. Thus among the three top reasons selected from our list by religious were growth in spirituality and relationship with God as well as the desire to live in religious community. The answers of the lay people were more likely to point to aspects of the ministry, their personal and family needs, and, given how much lay persons are directly recruited by pastors who know them, this relationship to the pastor. Thus the reasons most often cited by the lay people were such ministry motives as a "call to church service," and the desire to "serve people," and "be part of church life in a more active way," as well as the pastor's invitation and the fact that "the job fit my needs." This is not to underrate the more directly spiritual motivations of lay people--many did see the entrance into church ministry in terms of their relationship with God and their spirituality--but it was more church than personal and communal spirituality that dominated their motives.

Some pastors like to hire people into part-time positions, perhaps because the work requires only that (though most of the part-timers talk about working many more hours than agreed), perhaps because it is cheaper (especially if they are not paying health benefits), and perhaps because there is less of a management challenge in having part-time ministers than full-time ministers. As we have seen, two-thirds of the lay parish ministers (and even more of the part-timers) are married, most of whose husbands' incomes and medical coverage are apparently the primary family supports. We have noted that about ten percent are divorced and separated. For these ministers the parish often serves as the first site for returning to paid employment.

A few examples of how lay people gradually took on positions in parish ministry might be illuminating. One parishioner first volunteered in a variety of capacities, then became a secretary, and wound up the DRE in the parish. In another parish the cook accepted the pastor's invitation to become a youth/family minister, preparing weddings and working with youth religious education. One liturgy coordinator got into that position after expressing her disappointment with the way her child's first communion had been celebrated. Or another from our site observer:

> *Ms. A had volunteered in a number of ways in her parish: helping the school, serving as Eucharistic minister, working on a number of committees. Otherwise she was a typical Sunday Catholic, often planning the family menus during Mass in her inner city parish. She had what can be called a "conversion experience" while assisting with the catechumenate and now her spiritual journey, with the help of a sister who serves as her spiritual director, has become of utmost importance to her. She was invited to join the staff by the pastor and a pastoral minister who used to be at the parish and is now called "Parish Life Coordinator." Married with seven children, she has taken college courses in youth ministry and religious education with tuition assistance from the diocese and, as one can imagine, experiences considerable conflict between the ministry position that has her at the parish seven days a week and her family obligations. She has no ministry description but serves in a wide variety of ways from baptismal preparation of parents to managing the parish food bank to overseeing maintenance.*

It was evident from our site visits that many pastors seem to like having parishioners on staff not only because they cost less, but because they are committed to that particular parish, and know the people and situations of the parish. The ministers themselves who are parishioners seem, on balance, to think they have an advantage being parishioners for the same reasons, though they also find it largely impossible to draw a line between their staff role and their lives as parishioners. Other parishioners feel free to call upon them at any time. Thus, some spend many hours doing parish work (some said as many as 80 hours a week). Some resent this loss of privacy and personal time and the expansion of work hours. In two instances, they also noted that by being a parishioner-minister they no longer had a pastor: they could not look to the pastor for pastoring and spiritual ministry for themselves.

There are obvious problems with the hiring of parishioners: (1) they are harder to fire since they are parishioners (one pastor spoke of a youth minister-parishioner he had let go, but who remains in the parish, a source of discontent among those who support him); (2) they usually have some people in the parish whose feelings are less than positive toward them; (3) they are typically not as well trained for ministry; and (4) the fact that lines between their parishioner status and ministry roles are hard to draw. Some pastors make up for the initial lack of training, providing financial support from the parish for ministerial training. Others are less thoroughly committed to such development. One pastor expressed his disappointment that these ministers do not continue to volunteer for help beyond their new position, as much as some other parishioners who are also working forty hours in their employment.

The advantages and disadvantages of serving in one's home parish can also be seen in the experience of one pastor serving in his home parish where his mother still lives. He reports the advantage of knowing so many people and the history and dynamics of the parish, but also the confused relationships of serving as pastor to those who know him as neighbor. In still another of the parishes we visited, a newly appointed co-pastor had already been there, had grown up in the parish and still had family and many friends there. This gave him ready access to many groups in the parish and elicited considerable support. At the same time, the priest already there suddenly found himself a bit of an outsider to this leadership group of his co-pastor with his sister and friends.

Whatever one thinks about the idea of drawing on parishioners or about the other personal routes by which people become ministers of parishes, these entry routes into parish ministry are commonplace, and will probably become only more prevalent, and the diocesan policies and other procedures will simply have to adjust. Furthermore, though people begin as parishioners, they often become "professional" in some sense and, of course, it behooves the parish and diocese to help them do so by providing education and training. Then, whether with the hiring pastor or even more with his successors, these people have a double claim on the position--that of parishioner and that of "professional." One of our observers put it well:

In the two parishes visited it was clear that every parish has a personality and life of its own. Each parish's life continues as pastor and lay ministers come and go. Pastors have significant effect but increasingly the lay ministers are significant contributors to that life and personality. In the case of St. A, the staff (except for one) all came from the parish. In a future pastoral change, a new pastor will not be able to dismiss lay ministers who come from the parish as easily as those who are "outsiders." As those lay ministers become more experienced and competent (assuming there is support for their professional development), any conflict between staff and new pastor will be more difficult to resolve. Parishes will also lose the valuable experience of ministers coming from other situations if pastors increasingly hire from within the parish.

The sisters in parish ministry come through a variety of routes. Almost half (44 percent) come via their congregation's clearinghouse services or contacts or through diocesan clearinghouse efforts. Very few (less than 2 percent) come via national sources--newspaper ads or organizational networks. Almost a quarter (23 percent) of them wind up at a parish through personal contact with parishioners, staff members, or the pastor. The route to the parish can have many variations on these themes. *In one parish, the pastor arranges with the order for retired sisters (at this time the parish has one who is 76 and another who is 80) who are expected both to do ministerial activity... and to go fishing with him. Another arranges for the order to encourage sisters to come to the parish. Other sisters have been co-workers or friends of the pastor in the past. In one case, such a pair of friends was appointed as a pastor-pastoral assistant team by the bishop. (Simply because the pastor may have known sisters from earlier associations and have invited them to work in the parish does not mean that they are assured a friendly or peer-like association: in one parish where the pastor recruited two sisters he had known, he not only maintains a clearly hierarchical and formal relationship--he insists that they call him "Father" and bans any small talk around the rectory. He admits to having brought them to the parish only because he thought that parishioners would respect them more than they would a lay person.) Still others write to all the people they know looking for a position. Some few are looking for a position near a parent or parents whom they must care for. One sister was assigned as pastoral administrator after her provincial had a meeting with the bishop to explore possible positions in the diocese for her sisters.*

Almost all of the sisters (93 percent) have had experience in school ministry (while 46 percent of the lay persons have had school teaching and or/administrative experience).[23] Some pastors find that this school background is especially helpful if the ministers are working with religious education and/or youth ministry. Given the enormously positive feelings that prevail regarding the contributions of former teachers to these new parish ministries, obviously most have made the transition successfully. Yet for some former teachers the transition from school ministry to general parish ministry is not an easy one. In the school, their responsibilities were clear, days and weeks were well scheduled, the success of their efforts was measured concretely in test results, and the teacher had to do little or nothing to attract children to the classroom. On the contrary, in parish ministry, responsibilities can never quite be nailed down in a job description even if one exists, the work spills across the hours of the day and the days of the week, it is difficult to know the results of one's work, and the ministers must work to attract people to the community and ministry of the parish. *One pastor described a situation in which some of the responsibilities he thought he had assigned to Sister____ were not being carried out. He suggested that Sister _____ had come from a school background where the structure clearly indicates what needs to be done. "In parish ministry, especially at St. A_____, creativity and initiative are needed. Much of what the pastoral minister is called to do has not been done before or is uncharted territory." Another youth minister we visited, who had been a school teacher most of her life, had decided that the change was too drastic for her and that she needed to return to the much more orderly and controlled context of the classroom. In another parish we visited, the parishioners spoke of a lay parish minister who had been long in school ministry and who treated the parishioners like schoolchildren.* While the vast majority with a school background make the adjustment, some simply do not and many probably undergo some difficulties of adjustment in the first year or so.

*   *   *

In closing this section, we should note that the majority of pastors seem to be looking for people who can combine personal and ministerial abilities. One observer reports the intention (and obvious success) of a pastor who said he was looking for people of strong faith, who had "people skills" and competence in their own line of work. *He said he liked to have people work first on a volunteer basis, for both of them to find each other's particular way of working. He used the term "collaboration" and described it as respecting the views of others and utilizing the strengths of each person. This was exactly what I found evident in talking with the staff.*

A valuable insight was offered by one of our observers regarding the personal/ministerial balance in hiring a minister. *He reports that when the position of the person is relatively clear and well understood, such as that of a director of religious education, one might stress the competence in those educational and administrative skills. When the position is far from clear, however, and the responsibilities of "pastoral ministers" or "pastoral associates" are not clear, then personal qualities are more important as is support from the pastors until the person develops a relationship with the parishioners and has a "track record."*

One other point worth noting: increasingly, councils and their committees or other committees of parishioners play a role in the hiring and contribute to defining both the position and the qualifications. They seem to be as concerned as pastors with a balance between relational qualities and ministerial competence. One woman on a parish interviewing committee said the first criterion that she looked for in a candidate was that "they fall in love with us."

The future profile of parish ministry will be quite different as the number of sisters available declines and perhaps the level of education of the ministers declines. More than one diocesan official has forecast another problem: the disappearance of lay people with good theological and ecclesial preparation--ex-sisters, Catholic school graduates, etc.--for ministry.[24] Just as seminaries must do remedial "socialization" of seminarians, so will dioceses have to socialize people into practical Catholic ecclesiology.

One final comment: though many lament the withdrawal of women religious from parochial schools and undoubtedly they are sorely missed, clearly the pastors of the parishes felt the need of these women in other parish ministries as well. The readiness of sisters to take on new ministries to meet these needs has been an important contribution to parish life. They did so in uncertain circumstances, going into uncharted waters, and steering a new course, not without difficulties. In the process they are helping to reshape parish ministry to meet the new conditions and needs of ministry.

IV: Roles and Activities of the Ministers

As we will see, in one sense each pastoral ministry position seems unique: each pastor and staff decide the particular configuration of responsibilities that will constitute the job description--formal or informal--of each minister. There can be an almost idiosyncratic character to each person's role: combining any variety of tasks depending on the needs of the parish and the interests of the pastor and/or the pastoral minister. The following account of a parish minister may not be the best to indicate the uniqueness and complexity of parish ministers' roles, but it will do especially when one considers that this person works only **part-time** and in what could at first blush seem to be a very restricted role indeed, that of a minister to the sick in the parish.

> *Ms. N., minister to the sick and shut-ins, has been a part of the parish staff for six years, is scheduled to work part-time (20 hours), and receives a stipend of $170.00 a month and a $50.00 a month allotment for gas. Her primary responsibilities include: being aware of who is sick in the parish; organizing teams to visit the sick; advising the parish priests who is in need of critical care and a visit from the priests; scheduling 100 Eucharistic ministers to serve at weekend liturgies; training Eucharistic ministers; leading communion services in the church when a priest is not available; visiting the sick in a nursing home and the hospitals weekly; attending wakes; and following up the sick when they leave the hospital.*
>
> *What makes Ms. N.'s role more interesting is that many people come to her home in time of need; she sometimes feels that her home is like the rectory in this respect.*

Though we wish to stress the uniqueness of almost every individual's position-- which will be underscored when we review the activities associated with each role-- there are clear patterns of staffing and clear trends in these patterns. The table indicates the various ministry positions and their relative prevalence in U.S. parishes.

The ministry with the longest history (other than that of musician), the most established support structure of degree-granting and certifying programs, and the best established need, that of religious education is obviously the most prevalent. When we combine the three basic positions in our list (DRE, CRE, and Adult Education), they account for 41.7 percent of all the parish ministers. We have also analyzed the profiles of those who have the title of "catechumenate directors" to see whether it makes more sense to merge them with the directors of liturgy or those of religious education and determined that they fit best with the religious educator for further analysis. (We should also point out that responsibility for the catechumenate seems,

MINISTRY ROLES OF LAY AND RELIGIOUS MINISTERS
(percent in study sample)

POSITION	Religious	Lay	Total
Pastoral Administrator	1.50	0.4	0.8
General Parish Minister	48.3	12.6	27.4
Director of Religious Education	27.2	27.9	27.6
Coordinator of Religious Education	3.5	18.6	12.3
Adult Education Director	2.5	1.4	1.8
Catechumenate Director	1.2	1.4	1.3
Liturgy Director	0.7	1.6	1.2
Music Director/Musician	1.2	12.5	7.8
Liturgist/Music Director	1.5	3.5	2.7
Social Ministry Director	3.7	1.6	2.5
Spirituality Minister	0.2	0.2	0.2
Youth Minister	0.0	12.8	7.5
Elderly Minister/Home Visitor	4.5	0.2	2.0
Minister to the Sick	1.7	0.0	0.7
Evangelization Minister	1.0	0.2	0.5
Business Manager	0.2	3.7	2.3
Other	0.7	1.6	0.4

aside from any title, is to be found almost equally among liturgists, religious education directors, and general parish ministers.) General parish ministers, including both those who are called pastoral associates and those who called themselves parish or pastoral ministers, are the next most prevalent group. Next in freqency are the music directors or musicians, then the youth ministers. The final group distinguishable and barely large enough to analyze separately are the liturgists. These include those who have responsibility for both liturgy and music and in total account for almost four percent of the parish ministers. The spread of other ministry positions, though not amounting to a large percentage of all parish ministers, is further evidence of the variety of ways parishes are staffed. We call these the "others."

Throughout this report, we will distinguish among the various ministers by role within the following categories:

(1) General parish ministers (including those labelled as such
     and the pastoral administrators)
(2) Religious Educators (including both DREs, CREs, and those
     responsible for adult education and for the catechumenate)
(3) Liturgy director or liturgists (including those responsible
     for liturgy and music)
(4) Music ministers
(5) Youth ministers
(6) Other (all the remaining ministers)

We should note that some of the total numbers of these separate roles are not large and the inferences we draw should be considered in this light. The total number of liturgists is only 38, of youth ministers only 73, and of music ministers only 76. Nonetheless, as the reader will see, the occupants of these roles emerge with sufficiently distinct profiles as to warrant their separate treatment.

Put another way, the percent of parishes with each of the most popular positions is as follows:

	Pct. of all parishes with lay/religious ministers
Religious Educator	75.7
General Pastoral Minister	24.5
Musician/Music Director	17.8
Youth Minister	14.9
Liturgy/Liturgy-Music Coordinator	10.0
Other	16.0

The patterns of staffing appear to be shifting, however, in recognizable forms though not at the same pace in all parishes, dioceses, or regions of the country. Many parish ministers who have once served as DREs, or would have done so, now find a broader role more satisfying; many pastors--for a number of reasons--are substituting parishioners for professionally educated and degreed religious educators. In doing so, the pastors often define the role more narrowly. Many parishes are finding it better to have a generalist on staff such as the "pastoral associate" or "pastoral minister" which together have become the second most prevalent role.[25] Moreover, tightened budgets are causing some parishes to hire fewer specialists and to count on pastoral ministers to cover a variety of responsibilities.

Another explanation for the shift from religious educators to general parish ministers was offered by one diocesan official. He explained that church ministers find the role of pastoral associate or parish minister more attractive than that of DRE:

"There is greater fulfillment as pastoral associate than as DRE. One is able to establish better relationships with people and feels more appreciated. The pastoral associate is dealing with people who have needs and welcome their presence. They don't have to face groups of kids who don't want to be there."

Furthermore, some dioceses and parishes report difficulty in finding qualified directors of religious education.

A good example of the proliferation of lay ministries is the Diocese of St. Cloud: in 1971 there were 15 DREs, no youth ministers, no pastoral ministers. Today there are 91 DREs, 17 professional youth ministers, and 15-20 pastoral associates, and the position of liturgist is beginning to emerge in some large parishes. St. Cloud is primarily a rural diocese.

Naturally enough, holders of some of the ministry positions--other things such as personal relationships, being equal--seem to enjoy more authority than others. They seem to more clearly approximate the status once reserved to the priests than others. This became clear in our site visits and other consultations. In general, those positions occupied more by women religious than by lay persons, the positions and ministers with more education, those that relate more directly to the pastor, and those that work more directly with the adults of the parish seem to be marked by more "status" in the parish as well as by somewhat higher levels of satisfaction among the ministers. This means that the general parish ministers, which meet all these conditions and who tend to be older as well, enjoy more status and satisfaction than many other ministers.

The position of music minister or music director requires some special consideration below.

Two other positions are worth special mention, though their numbers are still small and one of them does not even appear on the chart. These are the pastoral administrators--those who substitute for a resident priest pastor--and the parish business managers or administrators where there is a resident priest pastor.

There are only eight of the former, the surrogate "pastors," in our sample. It is difficult to tell whether this is the frequency one should expect; this would extrapolate to about 160 in the country, a number that is somewhat lower than the two hundred or more a few other researchers have estimated, but no one has solid information about the numbers. All prevailing estimates are inferential, based on incomplete reports from what might well be unrepresentative samples of dioceses and parishes. We do not offer much analysis of this role on the basis of these few instances, though this important role will require increased attention by many dioceses in coming years. We will generally regard it more appropriate to this report's purposes to incorporate these ministers into the "general pastoral minister" category in our analysis as some of those with general pastoral responsibilities. That the majority are religious squares with other research.

A more prevalent role, occupied by women in our site visits, is the one of business manager or administrator of the parish. These people can have considerable influence on the culture and process of the parish, on the behavior of the pastor who comes to depend on them, and on the lives of the others working in the parish. *As one pastor put it, "She really runs the place."* (Sometimes, this key administrative role between the pastor and other staff members is played by a general pastoral minister, in which case the person is most likely a sister. Here we are talking for the most part of one in the distinct role of manager or administrator, though what we have to say would usually apply to the general pastoral minister as well, *mutatis mutandis*.) Perhaps these are today's version of the "first assistant" of old. *The description of one such person by one of our observers is illustrative:*

> *Mrs.R. is the business administrator of the parish. For three years she was a part-time bookkeeper, working one day a week. Three years ago, the new pastor asked her to become the full-time parish administrator. She now prepares the budget, tracks the cash flow, pays the bills, keeps the payroll, does the hiring, firing, and supervision of all the lay employees, and develops their job descriptions. She schedules and does all the paper work for weddings, funerals and other sacramental events. She manages the records: sacramental, contributions, census. She has switched the whole operation to computers and has total disdain for the diocese because of its lack of help to her. She claims to have an extremely good working relationship with the pastor and they enjoy mutual and total trust, fully in tune with one another about the future direction of the parish. She says the pastor is absolutely the boss, but that it's okay that they don't always agree. She is married to a retired army officer who is still doing well as an executive in a defense-related company. Her children are grown. She is quite open about her love for the pastor and the parish and it was clear that they are good friends: she and her husband socialize with him frequently.*

For the most part, these persons are described favorably: they seem to improve the organization and follow-through of the pastor, they seem to help other staff members relate to the pastor and to get what they need for their work, and in a number of instances they provide affirmation and encouragement to the rest of the staff. In some cases, these people are seen to have a deleterious effect on the parish, exerting too much authority and control, giving too much weight to financial, managerial, or other factors regarding pastoral concerns.

To move beyond the titles, what do the parish ministers do? Almost three-quarters of the ministers have job descriptions although many would attest that they are less than accurate. The fewer the ministers and the closer the working relationship between the pastor and minister in these situations, the less important perhaps are the job descriptions as the ministers share broad responsibilities with the pastor. Nonetheless, there are some general patterns to the positions.

We asked those we surveyed whether they had **"leadership"** responsibility for various ministries and, if not, whether their position called for them to **"participate"** in that ministry or if it was simply not part of their responsibility (we also provided for the possibility that a certain ministry was not carried on in the parish). Besides the responsibilities that emerged from their responses, we can also sketch some other features of each type of minister. If we look at the full-time ministers first, the following picture emerges (we will describe below how part-time ministers in each category differ from full-timers).

General Pastoral Ministers

There is no ministry for which more than half these ministers are **leaders**, but nearly half have leadership responsibility for home visiting (49 percent), small group prayer and reflection (48 percent), ministry to elderly (48 percent) and religious education (43 percent). When we combine leadership with participation in a ministry a more typical picture merges. Roughly three-quarters are involved in:

Ministry	Pct. Involved
Home visiting	83.9
Social service	79.2
Ministry to the elderly	77.3
Evangelization	76.3
Ministry to the bereaved	74.9
Prayer/reflection groups	74.8
Administration-organizing	73.0
Religious education	72.0
Ministry training	70.6

Furthermore, almost two-thirds or more are involved in caring for the sick (66 percent), counseling of parishioners (63 percent) and the catechumenate (62 percent).

As is evident from this profile, the emergence of the general pastoral minister is often not an alternative to the work of religious education as much as an expansion of the work to include other ministries with religious education. Yet, it must also be said that some ministers' apprehensions that the new titles of "pastoral associate" or "pastoral minister" are simply hiding the old responsibility of religious education are not groundless.

General pastoral ministers are four times more likely to be religious than lay, which also means that they are mostly women, and that they are older than the other ministers. Almost a quarter of them are lay persons, more married women than single or male. They are well educated, the best educated among the lay ministers. These ministers are the ones who feel closest to God of all the ministers, which is significantly related to the fact that the majority are religious, for in general the religious report feeling closer to God than do their lay counterparts. They feel close to the church but the strength of this is notably less than their relationship to God. This is also reflected in the fact that they are somewhat more likely to see themselves as "minister of the Gospel" rather than "minister of the church." Among all the ministers they are also the ones who feel closest to both the parish and the pastor. We will discuss further on what they are looking for in staff relationships and interaction.

Among the part-timers, there are more lay people than religious and they tend to be a little older than the full-time general parish ministers and almost all of them are married. Since for these part-timers this is not a full-time career, it is not surprising that they have somewhat less education. Since they are working in their own parishes, it is not surprising that they feel somewhat closer to the parish than the full-timers do, though their relationship to the pastor is little different from the full-timers. The profile of responsibilities parallels that of the full-timers, though their leadership is more restricted especially to religious education, the catechumenate, and ministry training in particular. They are also more likely than the full-timers to share responsibility for youth and young adult ministry.

Religious Educators

There is a tendency in the field of religious education to make a sharp distinction between **directors** of religious education and **coordinators**, the former typically people with professional degrees in the subject, the latter less professionally equipped. For our purposes, because we could not rely on the significance of the titles, we have found it useful to consider these roles together.

Obviously, almost all of these persons (95 percent) have leadership responsibility for religious education. Furthermore there is no other ministry for which more than half exercise leadership. When we combine leadership and participation in a ministry, three-quarters or more are involved in:

Ministry	Pct. Involved
Religious education	97.0
Administration-organizing	76.4

When we look at other ministries for which they have leadership or some responsibility, they include: prayer and reflection groups (69 percent); evangelization (64 percent), ministry training (62 percent), liturgy planning and development (61 percent involved); the catechumenate (more than a third with leadership and almost two-thirds--61 percent--involved in some way); and youth and young adult ministry (55 percent, half of whom have leadership responsibility for this).

The religious education directors are more lay than religious, have the longest tenure, and are almost as well educated as the general pastoral ministers, which is well educated indeed. Among the lay people, two-thirds are married, two-fifths are in their forties, and almost all of them have had some experience as volunteers. They are also somewhat more likely to see themselves as ministers of the Gospel than of the church, more directed toward fostering relationships with God than with the church. About a quarter of them learned of their position through the diocesan office, but more of them learned of the position from the pastor or someone else in the parish or from a parish bulletin ad.

Among the part-timers, as was true of the general pastoral ministers, the vast majority are parishioners: lay, married women who are a little younger than the women in the broader position of general pastoral ministers. Almost half are in their forties. They have less education than their full-time counterparts, yet more than half are college graduates and half of these have master's degrees. In fact, almost half of them have a background as teachers. They have somewhat more of a church orientation to their ministry than their colleagues. The profile of their responsibilities parallels that of the full-timers, though as a group their work is somewhat more limited, which is to say that slightly fewer of them are involved in each of the ministries and significantly fewer of them are involved in ministry training.

Liturgists

Liturgists are a small group (about 4 percent of parish ministers) and rather young with three-quarters falling between the ages of 30 and 50. Their youth, in part, is explained by the fact that almost four in five are lay, who tend to be younger as a group.

The majority of liturgists are women, lay women (58 percent of all liturgists). A little more than half the liturgists are married, but more strikingly, about 22 percent are divorced or separated--more than twice the proportion of religious educators, the second highest group. As we will see, liturgists tend to be the most disgruntled parish ministers. For now, it will suffice to say that they are the only group that reports growing distant from God over the last five years. During that time they have grown distant from the church as well. Though it should be noted that more than three in four attest to receiving sufficient support, the number that claim support from the pastor is also low compared with other groups.

Because of its specialized nature, training in liturgy is commonly found at the graduate level and is one reason for the high level of education within the group. More than half (52 percent) have obtained a master's degree or better and another quarter have completed some graduate work.

Their specialization in training is reflected in their limited areas of involvement in the parish. The only activities three-fourths of them **lead** are those directly related to their area of expertise: planning (90 percent), leading (77 percent) and performing/conducting the music (77 percent) for the liturgy. The only other area they have a large leadership role in is ministry training (58 percent). Combining leadership and participation mostly reinforces their areas of concentration. Three-quarters of the ministers are involved in the following:

Ministry	Pct. Involved
Liturgy planning/development	100.0
Liturgy leadership	96.8
Liturgical music: perform/conduct	93.5
Ministry training	87.1

Youth Ministers

We have already noted that half the youth ministers are men, young men, whose future in the ministry seems very limited. Almost half are thirty or younger and almost 85 percent are below forty. Almost two-thirds are single and 85 percent are college graduates, a third of whom have master's degrees.

Aside from their lead role with the young (100 percent), youth ministers also take a lead role in religious education (80 percent). Combining leadership and participation broadens their area of ministry considerably: about three-fourths of youth ministers are involved in the following activities:

Ministry	Pct. Involved
Youth/young adult ministry	100.0
Religious education	100.0
Ministry training	78.2
Evangelization	76.1

They feel the least close to God, the church, and the parish (but remember how high a percentage are men). They have the shortest tenure, more than a third a year or less, and are more likely than others to be on the brink of leaving their current positions. Among all the ministers, they are the most likely to have found their position through a diocesan office, though even in their case, this is the exception rather than the rule.

They seem to derive neither the satisfaction, support, nor income necessary to keep them in this ministry. Furthermore, there is a lore about youth ministers that the almost complete availability young people expect of them dooms them to early burnout.

Music Ministers

The profiles of liturgists and music directors/ministers resemble one another since their roles tend to overlap. In fact, two-thirds of those grouped as liturgists claim both titles. Both groups are largely young and largely lay, but the music ministers are even more so. Half the full-timers have not passed the age of 40 and almost three-quarters (73 percent) are 55 and under, 85 percent are lay. But unlike the liturgists, most of the laity are men (55 percent): the only ministry group where lay men are a majority.

They are about as well educated as the liturgists, a little less than half (46 percent) with at least a master's and nearly three in five having had some graduate work. Most are married (59 percent) and a third have never married.

As expected, music ministers are heavily involved (96 percent or more) in all areas related to liturgy, though only in performing musically do they take a lead role more than half the time (96 percent). They are also highly involved in the catechumenate as evidenced in the following table:

Ministry	Pct. Involved
Liturgy planning/development	100.0
Liturgical music: perform/conduct	100.0
Liturgy leadership	96.1
Catechumenate	96.1

The only other areas involving half or more are ministry training and administrating/organizing (65 and 50 percent, respectively).

Apparently, music ministers relate better to pastors than do liturgists: 4 percent more claim to be at least "close" to the pastor. But more telling is the strength of that relationship: nearly twice as many music ministers as liturgists report being "very close." A larger percentage of music ministers also claim pastor's support (85 percent vs. 77 percent).

Other

The overwhelming majority of these ministers are women religious (84 percent) although the ratio of religious to lay is somewhat less dramatic among part-timers. Being mostly religious they are somewhat older: three-quarters above the age of fifty and a fourth above age 65. They are better educated and closer to God, church and parish than any other ministers and claim to be close to the pastor (65 percent) and supported by the pastor (88 percent) more frequently as well. They are probably the most content group in the study, though they are admittedly only a "group" because we have assembled them as such.

The profile of all these ministers gives some general impression of ministerial priorities, those ministries for which parishes are assigning some staff time and salaries. No ministry is so common and particular to all that more than two-thirds exercise leadership. Home visiting (62 percent), ministry to the elderly (62 percent) and social service (54 percent) come close. When we combine leadership and participation, however, about three-quarters of the ministers are involved in the following areas:

Ministry	Pct. Involved
Ministry to the elderly	79.4
Ministry to the bereaved	74.3
Evangelization	71.8
Social service	71.7

Other prevalent ministries are the following: counselling (69 percent); care of the sick (64 percent); social action (62 percent); and prayer and reflection groups (56 percent).

We began this chapter with the acknowledgment that each ministry position is almost unique. The profiles of the separate ministries could suggest the contrary. There is still a considerable amount of variation hidden within this apparent uniformity, especially since the separate profiles stress those activities that are commonplace in each ministry, leaving aside the activities that are not widely shared and that do reflect the peculiarities of each parish. The profiles also make evident, within the limits of our data, some trends: the preponderance of religious among the "new" general parish ministers; the breadth of responsibilities of these general parish ministers; the youth, short tenure, and unusual presence of men among the youth ministers; and the special tensions that seem to arise for the ministries that may well most bear traditional traits of a profession, namely, liturgy and music. Each of these trends warrants attention. Will we have enough lay persons with the experience and background needed for the growing number of general ministry positions? Are there ways to engage men in ministry for longer periods than at present? How can the contribution of liturgists and musicians to the joint efforts of all the priests and parish ministers be facilitated and made more satisfying to all? We will be touching on these and other questions further in the subsequent chapters.

V: Pastor-Pastoral Minister Relationships

All involved in the emergence of these new ministers will cite the leadership and disposition of the pastor as perhaps the single most significant factor. Actually this development has resulted from a combination of pastoral pragmatism of enterprising pastors, and ministerial initiative by dedicated religious and laity. While some pastors point to the symbolic value of adding women, and in fewer instances lay or religious men, to the leadership of church ministry, most were simply trying to assure basic ministry for parishes, traditional ministry such as religious education and care of the sick, attention to the new needs of the elderly and the bereaved, as well as the new demands of the catechumenate and sacramental preparation in general. This pastoral commitment of pastors combined with the readiness of lay people and religious to embark on new roles in the church has led to a considerable expansion or multiplication of ministries. At a time when shortages of priests and increasingly relative shortages of funds might warrant contraction of parish ministry, quite the opposite has taken place--a significantly more complex approach to sacramental preparation and celebration and the addition of many new ministries.

The other side of this initiative of the pastor is the considerable autonomy of each pastor. Within the limits of canon law (and, we are coming to appreciate, civil law as well), each pastor has enormous freedom regarding the ministries and structures of the parish: what positions he will have, what qualifications will be insisted on for each position, all the personnel conditions of employment. Further, what is autonomous can also be arbitrary and we will have to consider this implication of the present state of affairs. Yet, almost all the developments of parish ministry, then, depend on the judgment and initiative of pastors or at least on their willingness to entertain new prospects for parish life in response to the initiative of the lay and religious ministers or of parishioners.

These additions to the ministry staff have brought dramatic changes in the life and ministry of the priest himself. Most of the priests, who as pastors have hired parish ministers, began their ministry in a rectory-home where the only other pastoral minister might be a fellow priest and the only other employees might be cooks or housekeepers. They were assured the privacy that went with their celibacy and had little or no responsibility for what might be called personnel management, to say nothing of such concerns as "collaboration." There was also relatively little paper work, other than the maintenance and issuance of sacramental records, and consequently little need for any secretarial assistance. Now, these priests find that they live in a building that has become an office where there is not only secretarial help but where these new ministers' activities require accommodation of the space and time and activities that leaves them very little private "space" with the more than simply physical dimensions this word has come to connote. A small but increasing number of pastors is trying to segregate their residence from the work place of the parish, establishing offices in distinct sections of the rectory, in the schools, or in some other building, or setting up a residence apart from the rectory. Arrangements like these seem well called for as priests understandably seek ways not to lose all privacy, on the one hand, and to avoid the feeling of never being away from work on the other.

Support from Pastors

Few people in church circles have not heard stories of pastor-parish minister conflict, of arbitrary changes of ministry and terminations of ministers by new pastors, of pastors who have difficulty communicating with their staffs. What are remarkable, however, are not the examples of tension or of unwise behavior by pastors, but the extent to which these new ministers report good relationships with their pastors and good support from them. Among the full-time ministers, all but about 15 percent say that the pastor's support is adequate and even fewer feel somewhat distant from their pastors, nine out of ten say that the pastor is satisfied with their performance in ministry, and almost as many say they feel quite free to discuss their difficulties with their supervisors who are almost always the pastors.[26] We will examine a number of items that together detail the relationships between pastors and parish ministers (matters such as staff meetings, communication, decision making, etc.) but we also asked the ministers to choose a term that best characterizes this relationship for them. Here are the choices of all the ministers, full-time and part-time (arranged in an order from the most "equal" to the least "equal" relationship):

CHARACTERIZING MINISTERS' RELATION TO PASTOR
(percent)

Friend	5.9
Team member	24.4
Colleague	10.4
Staff member	36.0
Helper	4.6
Employee	15.5

The above responses total 96.8 percent. The remaining 3.2 percent of ministers selected both "friend" and another of the above choices to characterize their relationship with the pastor.

The more the parish ministers are indeed partners with the pastor, i.e., the more they share the broad range of ministry concerns as general pastoral ministers, the more they do feel like team members or colleagues: 45 percent of the full-time general pastoral ministers choose these terms. If we add "staff member," which in a list that includes "employee" suggests professional respect, the percentage of full-time general pastoral ministers who see themselves in professional working relationships climbs to 75 percent. Almost as many of the full-time religious educators find themselves in similar relationships with their pastors, and the same can be said of those in "other" ministries. If there have been difficulties in the relationships between pastors and lay parish ministers, it must be remembered, however, not only how ill-prepared priests were for this shift, but that this shift began to occur in the late "sixties," when along with the beneficial opening up of new opportunities for people came somewhat unrealistic expectations of full equality of authority and responsibility. It was a time when one midwest pastor who was among the first to develop a mixed staff that considered itself a "team," was heard to wonder: "Does team ministry mean that everybody gets to do what he or she likes and the pastor gets left to do the rest?" And an eastern pastor found in staff meetings that while everyone else could voice his or her opinion with vigor, when he did so he was accused of resorting to an old authoritarian model. *The Director of the Office of Ministry in the Archdiocese of St. Paul-Minneapolis has reflected on how the views and expectations of lay ministers have evolved:*

> *Ten years ago, all staff members were viewed equally. The pastor had no more authority than anyone else. Today there is a clearer recognition of the pastor's role. Fundamentally he is in charge and responsible. But this responsibility is borne in mutuality. However, where the pastor's power is used to negate the staff's efforts or undercut a staff person's own pastoral wisdom, then tension develops.*

Of course, pastors often inherit staffs from their predecessors. As we have noted, this transition is the occasion for many "horror stories" about peremptory changes by the new pastors, sudden firings, serious changes in the working relationships. Actually, while this sometimes is all too true, it was good to find it was not prevalent. We have no statistics on the incidence of these sudden and drastic dismissals, but the survey and our site visits give evidence of good, if sometimes difficult, transitions. Yet there is something in the situation which makes some difficulty not so surprising nor simply a matter of poor performance on the part of those involved.

If there has been a well-developed staff--of however small a number--it seems rather clear that, given the small size of parish staffs, this has undoubtedly entailed good personal relationships between the pastor and the rest of the staff; the better the staff, the more likely this is. If the previous pastor had himself hired the staff (and even more so had hired people he had known previously) the new pastor has quite a challenge on his hands as do the staff members. Any change is going to be difficult: a stranger is coming into the personal relationships of a small number of people. In some parishes, where the relationships of the staff to the previous pastor were essentially one-to-one relationships, rather than those of a group with each other, the challenge is even greater. *As we observed in one parish, a pastor with a strong organizational sense, and one who wants to develop the relationships of the group through staff meetings and other group efforts, can find the staff somewhat resistant to the change. The staff in this parish find the new pastor quite supportive of their work and the meetings he organizes and conducts very effectively make a great contribution to their mutual learning and cooperation in ministry. He may be a bit more controlling than some like, but his strategy may be necessary in situations where the previous pastor had built the staff around the personal loyalty of each minister to himself rather than to the group.*

Sometimes, the new pastor suffers from the "penny wise but pound foolish" practice of the former pastor, which can be a detriment to the quality of staff as much as it can be to the care of buildings. Regarding staff, this has meant in some instances hiring parishioners with very little training and on a part-time basis, leaving his successor with people who have neither the talent nor the time to provide help when and how it is needed. The successor then faces grave obstacles either in increasing the responsibilities of that staff because they have neither the time nor the talent to meet greater responsibilities, or in replacing staff who are dedicated parishioners.

Further flesh and blood can be added to the survey data from our site visits. As one can imagine, the relationships are enormously varied. One minister, a sixty-eight-year-old sister, says with satisfaction that "he tells me what he wants and I do it," but this deference creates a problem for the other sister on staff who feels that she should have her own well-defined areas of responsibility. Often the pastor has a relationship to each minister without bringing them together. Sometimes, the pastor seems to relate mostly to the support staff and leaves the pastoral staff to their own devices. When there are other priests on the staff, the pastor often seems to be the only one with a relationship to every "staff" member, priests and other pastoral ministers.

In this time of transition and innovation, where new positions and new relationships are being established, some pastors and pastoral ministers find it very helpful to clarify the relationships by spelling out job descriptions and through other structures, which we will describe in the next section. *Some pastors seem reluctant to clarify the relationships and expectations regarding the lay ministers; they want to be able to call upon the ministers for whatever they regard as needed. As one lay minister reported: "Clarity is not a goal of the pastor." Furthermore, some pastors in our study sites were reluctant to be forthcoming about their pleasure or displeasure regarding the ministers' work. In one parish, pastoral ministers often were told of the pastor's displeasure through a third person, leaving them to wonder about the accuracy of the report. In the instance of this parish and others, the other members of the staff repeatedly assured the observer that they think the pastor is a good person, even if he finds it difficult to achieve the kind of communication necessary for smoothly functioning relationships.*

In one midwestern parish that experiences continual staff turnover because of frustrations in communications with the pastor--his lack of affirmation, his apparent agreement with a consensus among the staff only to decide differently when he is away from them, his not consulting them about the building of new staff offices, hurting people's feelings at staff meetings (apparently without advertence), etc., etc.--our observer found: "All agree that the pastor is a good man, probably a saint. He is very difficult to work with!"

The pastors themselves can be rather ambivalent about the kind of relationship they want to establish with their staff members, an ambivalence perhaps built into the complex of personal and work dimensions of ministry we have already discussed. On the one hand, they can hire staff on a rather personal basis--people they know, feel they can relate well to, may have worked with before, as more important than professional training and experience; on the other hand they try to maintain some personal distance from staff members.

Most pastors seem to want relatively independent, rather task-oriented colleagues, while women, and women religious in particular, may talk more in terms of "interdependence."[27] Often this entails a more personalist framework for one's working relationships. Within such a framework, it can be difficult to understand or find comfortable so strongly a task-oriented relationship.

Although pastoral ministers might work rather independently, one important kind of support by pastors is, negatively, not to allow parishioners to go around them to the pastor, and, positively, to introduce pastoral ministers to various groups so as to underscore the legitimacy of their ministry. *In one rural parish where our observer found the pastor to be "a very gentle man, theologically well read, with a love for his ministry and for the people with whom he works, one who has deep regard for his staff," in this parish one pastoral minister said of him: "I have learned so much from him. When I came on staff he took me with him and introduced me to every shut-in and hospital person. They quickly accepted me, so that now it doesn't matter which one of us makes the visit."*

It is part of our current wisdom that men, and especially men in supervisory work situations, judge their relationships with those on staff, especially the women on their staff, as better than the staff members do. In fact, the relationships are better according to the criteria the men employ. This difference of perspective is naturally enough present among some pastors: they think relationships are better than the others do. More than two-thirds (67.4 percent) of the pastors in our survey described their relationships with the lay women on staff as quite close (1-2 on a scale of 5), while 10 percent fewer of the lay women saw the relationship in such positive terms. Furthermore, while almost 15 percent of the lay and religious ministers saw their relationship with the pastor as one of an employee, less than 2 percent of the pastors saw it that way; they preferred to see it as the relationship of colleagues or team members. Pastors (as may be true of all those in positions of authority) think they are more accessible, that there is more of a team approach, that relationships are more personal, than the others do.

An important distinction seems to be that between the structured relationships and supports of a pastor with the staff and the more personal qualities in these relationships. It often boils down to the quality of communication between the pastor and the parish ministers. There are many reports of pastors who are regarded as reasonably comfortable to work with, who give the individual considerable freedom for the exercise of ministry, and who establish adequate structures for the most part, and yet who are less than forthcoming in more personal terms: rarely offering words of affirmation or encouragement and reluctant to take on the kind of performance review that requires direct confrontation. A particularly poignant instance is reported by one of our observers:

Ms. T. indicated that she gets most of her satisfaction and recognition from parishioners. "Father is not very good at giving compliments." She shared a story of an evening of reflection she had recently facilitated for eucharistic ministers. When it ended, she asked Fr. T. "how it went." He said "it was great." She then indicated that she had expected some evaluation and constructive criticism of the various parts of the evening. (She said she never gets that kind of feedback from Fr. T. unless she specifically asks.)

She continued by telling me that a few days later in a Holy Thursday homily, Fr. T. included most of the points she had covered in the evening of reflection. When she heard him repeat these in his homily, "It blew me away. It was done so beautifully, it brought me to tears. I guess my interpretations were legitimate. I guess he accepted them." This was an indirect form of appreciation for her worth and expertise.

On Good Friday, she told Father, "You and I are very different people. That's okay, but I guess we are working toward a common goal. And we do have some cohesiveness. It's really difficult sometimes because you don't give affirmation. You don't indicate how you feel about things, but through your homily you indicated a tremendous amount of affirmation toward me. I thank you for that. Father T. responded by saying, "I don't affirm very often or verbalize my feelings. I usually say something when things go wrong." Then she said that he gave her a hug. "We're on the right track. We can work together," he said. She pointed out also that there were no comments on her annual performance review, just check marks. Even there he doesn't verbalize, she indicated.

The challenge for priests of working in more complex relationships with lay persons in ministry led one priest to comment:

There is a real need for leadership training for priests. Many men going into the seminary and those just beginning parish life were not mature enough, emotionally and otherwise, to understand the problems of parish life or to cope with what today's priesthood calls for. Seminary training puts too much emphasis on structure and not the kind of spiritual development or relational skills needed in working with people in the parish.

Actually, this may be a bit idealistic since there are many examples in our study of parishes where the pastor provides a framework or structure in which many ministers can work effectively without himself being particularly adept at relationships. In these parishes, pastors were convinced of the need for the ministries these ministers could provide. Whatever their personal feelings about the matter, these pastors were prepared to live with the fact that sometimes these other ministers were more competent than they in various areas, enjoyed better relationships among staff and with parishioners, and were more popular. *One pastor, by his own description and the confirmation of diocesan officers, had a history of finding competent people who could encourage parishioners to participate. He says that he looks for talent and then must not get into an attitude of competing with the others, even if they eclipse him in performance or popularity. He specifically told our observer, accurately, that one of the other priests was "clearly the most popular priest here." His own way of relating to people can be somewhat reserved, and one of the other staff talked of advising him when a staff member needs personal attention.*

Before discussing specific kinds of relationships related to status (clergy, religious, lay) and position, we might summarize what we have been saying in this way. The best kind of relationship is one that strikes a balance between cordiality and hospitality (as a general style and evidenced in easy access, informal contacts, etc.) on the one hand, and fairly good structures or procedures (job descriptions, staff meetings, joint planning), on the other, all with a rather clear understanding that the relationships exist for the sake of the ministry.

In some instances, a pastor-sister relationship has become strong and effective, a kind of "co-pastoring" relationship, even if not formally so called. Such co-pastoring relationships, whether they are literal and involve two priests or they are analogous and involve a priest with a sister or lay person, can be very supportive. *As one pastor who had been in a literal co-pastor situation with another priest reflected: "It's nice to be able to talk to a friend-fellow priest after a meeting or event, one who will appreciate what you have done. After all, praise is short-coming in our profession."* In these instances, it is easy to see the relationship to each other becoming as important as, respectively, his to other priests or hers to other religious. Diocesan and religious order (men and women) personnel directors need to be aware of this when they are making changes in ministry.

In one instance, the religious order put a new priest team in place of the priest who had a team relationship with a sister; the effect was that the sister became the odd person out in the new situation and, though everyone in the parish spoke with enormous enthusiasm about her abilities, she felt she had to leave for a new parish rather than settle for so much less a role in leadership. In another, a new bishop renewed the appointment of the pastor but refused to do so with the sister, even though his predecessor had appointed them both at the beginning. Tensions arise in situations where it is up to the priest involved to work out new collaborative relationships in ministry and then the diocese acts arbitrarily in the assignments of the priests without attention to the other ministers in a parish.

This challenge for diocesan and religious order personnel directors to respect ministerial relationships in a parish may be especially acute where pastoral administrators are primarily responsible for directing the ministry of a parish. This may even involve sensitivity regarding the agreed titles of those in ministry. In one case, the diocese refers to the priest as the "canonical pastor," but he is anxious to support the leadership of the woman carrying on the ministry there and calls himself the "sacramental celebrant." It is common in these situations to hear discussion about how important it is that the priest involved, as pastor or sacramental minister, make every effort to ensure that the parishioners understand who has the primary pastoring responsibility in the parish.

Another complex of relationships exists where there is more than one priest in a parish as well as parish ministers. This is true in larger parishes, as we have seen, and especially in parishes staffed by religious orders because they prefer to ensure religious community for their priests in parish work. As a matter of fact, we have found that where one might expect a problem for the pastoral ministers because the priests living together can communicate so much more with one another and feel so much more "ownership" of the parish ministry, in some instances the pastor often has a closer relationship with the pastoral ministers than with his fellow priests.

The dynamic of pastor-other priests relationships relative to the pastor's relationship with the lay parish ministers can be talked about also in terms of the position of priests who are associate pastors (parochial vicars, in the Code's term). Frequently, the associate pastor's relationships remain rather ambiguous. Typically, the associate pastor's role and responsibilities are the least well articulated. He seems to be able to move in any direction he finds comfortable. In some instances, he becomes the odd man out. He relates well to no one. He is neither lay nor religious, nor is he so clearly one of the pastor's own persons, since he was appointed by the diocese or order and not hired by the pastor. At other times, the associate pastor seems to pair up with one of the other ministers, a source of special support and encouragement. Obviously, the age of the associate affects much of this: if he is young and is not given clear areas of authority and accountability he can be treated somewhat as the youth minister; if he is older, he usually carves out a work-space for himself.

In some instances, it is the associate pastor who resents the intrusion of the lay/religious ministers into the living space of the rectory. *As one older priest asserted, the rectory is the priests' house and he doesn't want anyone else in it. He "can't stand having meals with the nuns and lay people because priest-talk is none of their business."*

To be sure, in some parishes, the lay person can come to be regarded as more important than a particular priest/pastor. *"We would be much worse off losing her than if the pastor were changed," was one illustrative expression of this.* Some pastors have heard such promotion of lay ministry and have grown to resent it, as if they were holdovers from another era. As one pastor put it:

> *There is so much talk about the time in the future when we won't have priests, so much talk that it is like a self-fulfilling prophecy. We can't run a church without clergy. The laity feel they can do it all and do it better. They have higher standards for priests than they do for themselves. This creates tensions. The lines are becoming blurred between the role of the priest and that of the lay minister.*

We now shift from relationships of people in various statuses to those involving various ministry responsibilities. As others take specific jobs in parish life, the pastor is asked to accommodate his behavior to meet the needs of that person and his/her work. While the tensions inherent in this can be present regarding any ministry, it becomes an especially acute problem, it seems, with liturgists and musicians. We will use that relationship to identify some of the dynamics.

First, the minister is a specialist with the specialist's criteria of what makes for good performance, while the pastor is a generalist and is expected to be an integrator, one who seeks to relate that specialized ministry to the other ministries and to the people who have more ordinary taste and customs to which the specialist must accommodate. *As one woman with professional training in liturgy and music and who is a liturgy and music coordinator in a parish reflected:*

> *I've had difficulties with the pastor and the liturgy commission [of the parish pastoral council] because of their determination to be welcoming to everyone. This has meant that they want more popular hymns and less frequently changed hymns, while I want to try new hymns and some that are more complicated.*

They also used more personal and informal greetings in the liturgy, invited people to hold hands at the Lord's Prayer, and invited individual petitions at the General Intercessions, all of which I thought compromised the more proper formality of the liturgy. I have learned in the process and it's better now, but we still have problems.

On the other hand, the pastor is used to acting alone and/or moving among a variety of ministries as they come up and can often neglect the preparation needed to cooperate with the specialist or, worse, think he can change things (hymns, procedures) at the last minute. As one observer found:

While staff meetings were held regularly, formal agendas were not always adhered to by the pastor. Staff members felt that when they prepared material for meetings and sent them to staff ahead of time, the pastor read them during the meeting and so wasn't prepared. The pastor on the other hand felt the religious education office made their decisions separately and then just informed the rest of the staff. He cited as an example the planning of a liturgy. The liturgy was designed and planned and then handed to the pastor to celebrate without his having an opportunity to have input into the decisions.

It seems that either we should start training priests to be the primary liturgical directors of parishes since they are going to lead the liturgy anyway and since it is so related to their priesthood, or priests without such expertise need to be able to acknowledge this. The present relationship between leadership and expertise lacks cohesion. One music minister seemed to confirm this somewhat. *After voicing his view that problems between musicians and pastors derive from the intransigence of opinionated music ministers or pastors, he said he regarded himself as expert in music but not in liturgy. He was prepared to concede to the pastor's judgment about what was best for the good of liturgy.*

But, as we said, this was but the most acute example of an inevitable tension, one caused not primarily by the personalities of those involved or any clericalism or anticlericalism, but by the different roles and backgrounds of those involved: the integrating generalist background and responsibility of the pastor and the professional background of the specialist minister.

To conclude this section before turning to a broader picture of staff relationships, we wish to repeat what we said at the beginning. There are difficulties to be worked out in the relationships between pastors and parish ministers, difficulties that can be framed as personnel matters, as ministerial-professional or generalist-specialist matters, as male-female relationships, as clerical-lay matters, or in still other categories. Each of these requires attention as we will propose further on. Yet, given all the personal, organizational, ecclesial, and cultural changes involved, it is a tribute to the church that the relationships are as good as they are. We will conclude this section with an appendix reproducing how some of our observers described the various styles of pastors who clearly enjoy good relationships with their parish ministers.

Appendix to Chapter Five

While we describe lay and religious parish ministers throughout this study, the following are the reports of our site visitors on some of the pastors who have worked out a good relationship with their lay and/or religious parish ministers.

1. Father A. has been in this parish in the northeast for four years and seems to love both being a pastor and being in this parish. Having served in the chancery with a licentiate in canon law, he is a well-read man. He doesn't seem to like too many structures: there are no staff meetings, no job descriptions or contracts with any of the staff (other than one for the pastoral associate sister because it was required by her order). He is extremely open and caring for his people. More than one person told me that when a person calls with a problem, his first response is to ask when it would be a good time for that person to talk with him; his calendar and schedule seemed to revolve around other people's needs. The real story of the parish is the great working relationships among this pastor, a priest associate, and a sister pastoral associate. They love and respect each other, they eat dinner together every day, pray together every day, and work very closely together every day. The two men truly believe that if a priest cares about the parishioners, it is important to have a woman as part of the leadership of the parish.

2. In discussing the staff of this parish in the west and lay ministry in general, Father B. the pastor was looking for people of strong faith, who had "people skills," and who were competent in their own line of work. He used the term "collaboration" regularly and described it as respecting the views of others and utilizing the individual strengths of each person. This was exactly what each of the other staff members confirmed as his approach. He recognizes that the laity bring certain gifts such as compassion, understanding, and greater vision of family needs and development. His chief concern was "youth leakage." He said this needed serious attention and at this time was asking himself how to deal with this problem. He was working on better children's liturgies and religious education programs.

3. Father C. in the farm belt stays current in pastoral matters: he has a good personal library in his office and reads ten periodicals regularly. He is very easy to talk to and comes across as a very pastoral individual. It is clear that he relies on others around him to do those things for which he is not particularly gifted. He has surrounded himself with very competent people and this is evident in the parish. The staff meet once a month in a meeting that includes: prayer, faith sharing, review of events each is responsible for, joint study of something that will help them all. They take turns chairing these meetings. Overall, the pastor seems to like and respect all the staff and the staff feel the same way about him.

4. Monsignor D. seems to delegate authority for day-to-day operations in this southern parish to the woman who serves as parish business manager. He regularly consults with the parish finance council on issues of money and seems to consult with the parish pastoral council on the development of new programs. He feels that this is his means of being accountable to the laity of the parish. He did not, however, consult the parish pastoral or finance council before hiring two lay people on a part-time basis for pastoral ministry to

the young and the sick. He takes great pride in the buildings of the church and parish hall. He is described by the parishioners as very warm and friendly. With the staff, he tends to be rather formal, but most of the staff regard their relationship with him as quite positive, and say that he gives them the support and freedom they need to carry out their responsibilities. The minister to the sick says that he is very responsive to her requests to provide pastoral care to those who need him. In fact, he did not initiate her ministry: she suggested it and he readily agreed. While the staff rarely meet together, rarely socialize, and never pray together, they seem to respect each other and enjoy each other.

5. Father E. has been a priest for thirty years. One's first impression is of a long, lanky, shy, somewhat uncoordinated man, even a bit clumsy. After a while his simplicity and straight talk win you over and you get the feeling that you've known him for a long time. He says he spends most of his time in this southwest parish on homily preparation, visiting parishioners, what he calls grief counselling, endless meetings, the lay leadership formation program, and general Hispanic evangelization. He is president of the diocesan pastoral council and takes an active part in any diocesan activity regarding Hispanics. He can't imagine being anything but a priest and loves this parish and especially the parishioners. He is a deeply spiritual man and had a great deal to say about how bad a job our church is doing with Hispanics.

6. Father F.'s warm pastoral and intelligent management style have earned everyone's respect and he is clearly considered the boss in this New England parish. He often takes the staff members out to dinner and attends social functions with them and their families, and they talk about enjoying his company. They all consider each other as friends. They have monthly staff meetings that the pastor chairs. They pray and play together on a fairly regular basis and about every other year they all go away for a couple of days to plan the work of the parish.

7. Father G. seemed smart and sensitive and happy with his pastoral work. His motto for getting along as a pastor is to "try to love the parishioners that fight you." In this southwest parish, there are staff meetings every other week with a well-organized agenda: each item has a time limit. The pastor and members of the staff take turns chairing, preparing the prayer, and serving as secretary. The pastor evaluates everyone annually and they in turn evaluate him.

8. Father H., the founding pastor of this midwest parish, has a background on the minor seminary faculty and with the Charismatic Renewal. He feels that his work with the CR and Cursillo and other renewal groups that were lay-run gave him the direction and formation for running a parish with its members, not paid staff, as ministers. He stated, "The people have to own the church. You can't have professionals doing it. My right hand isn't paid to be part of my body." The model he uses he calls "Spirit filled." When the church was built, 75 percent of the labor was provided by the parishioners. As pastor, he invests time in training the people either by his own teachings or by sending them to Steubenville for training or by having training teams come to the parish. The people love him, appreciate his gifts, and find him easy to work with. People are given room to do their work, whether they are the staff (who simply organize the parishioners' work) or the parishioners. His philosophy is "The important thing is the relationships rather than the task. If at the end of a meeting we do not love God and each other better, nothing matters."

9. Father I. in this northeast parish is vigorous, energetic, pastorally sensitive, has a sharp wit and uses it constantly. He makes fun of himself and uses humor to his best advantage. He is an engaging conversationalist, sure of himself, a man of strong convictions. His directness is surprising to people who had become accustomed to a lack of trust and directness in the previous pastor. The evening I arrived, he had already attended two wedding rehearsals and two wake services, and had gone to the hospital to see a retired priest in intensive care. The people talk of him as "willing to change," "open," "welcoming," "compassionate." He is a wonderful presider at a children's liturgy, preaching to the children and through them to the adults. He had an easy and friendly manner and knew most of the children by name. He works at being a pastor; he works at being open and forgiving; he works at being a good priest. The people have responded in kind. They volunteer to do anything that needs to be done and he affirms their gifts and welcomes them. His reputation in the town is that he welcomes all. In healing conflict in the parish, he listened a lot and moved slowly.

10. Father J. in this western parish was very open in his discussion of the staff and spoke mostly of their strengths. He used words like "tops," and "excellent," and "enthusiastic" to describe them.

11. Father K. in this rust belt parish is the charismatic pastor who creates much whirlwind in the parish. He is a nonstop, loosely organized person who is extremely verbal and humorous. He is supportive of the work of others but dislikes having meetings. He has worked on his leadership skills: specifically trying to improve his listening and communication skills.

12. An air of peacefulness and tranquility pervaded the rectory of this midwest parish, a certain sense of centeredness, peace, gentleness. After meeting Father L., the pastor, I realized that much of it was due to his personal style and his presence. He exuded these same qualities. This is his home town. He is a very gentle person, well read, theologically up-to-date. His love for his ministry and for the people he works with came through constantly. He also has obvious and deep regard for his staff and respects them very much. Several times he commented on an excellent piece of work one or another staff member had done. He described staff as "free of tensions with excellent working relationships. While each person has a job description all the jobs interrelate so that we have to collaborate." This view was confirmed by the other two staff members. They do not always see eye to eye but have enough respect for one another's expertise and ministry to tolerate differences. As one staff member put it: "I may not always agree with something Father proposes and I feel free to tell him that at a staff meeting where we can discuss our differences. But if that is what is decided, I will support it. At the same time, the pastor feels the same freedom with me. He doesn't always agree with some of the things I might decide to do, or ways of approaching my work, but he gives me the latitude to do it and supports, doesn't undercut me." The pastor has made it very clear, the staff member said, that if parishioners have a problem with a staff member, they must discuss it with the person involved and not "run to Father."

13. Father M. in this southwest parish seemed charming, extremely traditional, hospitable, and somewhat eccentric. The people really loved this guy. He's been there through it all, the good times and the bad times in their lives. The kids loved him. The men said his experience in the Navy in Korea made them feel that he is a man who knows what they

are going through. Parishioners raved about his liturgies because he puts on unusual productions. He uses various props in his preaching, is dramatic, and brings mariachi music into this Hispanic community Mass. He has himself done all the art for the church, which is quite lovely.

14. Father N. is a young, bilingual pastor, educated in Europe, living in an old, run-down parish house, in this poor midwest parish, where his living and office space run over into each other. Born in this town, he believes he is called to be here now. He has a gift for languages and speaks Spanish fluently. Conducting a meeting with parishioners to plan a festival, he clearly worked at supporting them in their ideas, acting as a coordinator for what they wanted to do.

15. Father O. is ordained thirty-six years and has had two diocesan-sponsored sabbaticals, the most recent studying base communities in Africa to discover their implications for his pastoral work. He is described by the people in this northeast parish as an enabler, a listener, caring and sensitive to their needs. A parish council meeting is chaired by the pastor who listens to each person on each agenda item.

16. In this his first parish as pastor, Father P. described his ministry style as "hands on," "involving people," and "letting go because I can't do it all." He makes sure that there are women on the staff for the purpose of modelling both male and female ministry. Needing to hire new ministers, he has developed personnel policies and has involved the staff and parishioners in both developing positions and conducting the interviews.

17. Father Q., ordained forty-three years ago, is open but controlling. The staff of this northeast parish does not have regular meetings but each meets regularly with Father Q. The parish does not want to have a parish council, as evident in the consultation with the parishioners, and so they do not have one. In communication with each staff person, the pastor is very sensitive to what each says and actively solicits the opinion of each. The pastor has been on every action committee in the city for equal opportunity; he has bailed people out of jail in the middle of the night when they couldn't make bail, has been honored by civic groups. Each member of the staff feels that s/he has the support of Father Q. and the authority to carry out his or her tasks. He has a winning smile and quick wit and a strong desire to make the lives of those around him better than he found them. He is physically present to every group that meets and every civic and interfaith group in the city. He coordinated the first ecumenical Thanksgiving dinner. He has a true social conscience and all speak of his dedication, integrity, love of God and of the people. Although he is controlling in a clerical sense, he is a warm human being, sensitive and caring. The people joke with him, call him by his nickname. The pastoral control seems to be his way of assuring that everything is taken care of and he feels responsible for everything. He is working with people who acknowledge his need to feel this way and who work happily in the situation. Collaboration is on the pastor's terms but if someone suggested another way, he would be open to it. Father Q. is acknowledged by the townspeople to be a leader in social concern.

VI: General Staff Relationships

Besides the pastor-parish minister relationships, there is the general pattern of staff relationships, made more important the larger the staff. What does each expect to be the nature and style of that relationship? What turns out to be the styles of relationship? Is the staff a kind of small community trying to develop not only ministerial relationships but spiritual and social ones as well? Or are the staff's relationships largely restricted to coordination of their work, whether in a very collaborative style or in a rather formal style in which each essentially acts on her or his own?

Obviously, the permutations are endless. Just as obviously, the size, complexity, and organizational style of parish and staff make an enormous difference. *The highly organized staff arrangements we found in one parish are part of a whole style in which the parish reports having office hours and answering service, a formal planning process, clearly articulated mission statement, a pastoral council, a finance council, a separate "building commission" to plan future construction, a well-organized stewardship program in which 65 percent of the parish participate, use of a planning consultant from the "human resources" field and numerous organized ministries. It is not surprising then that this parish has an administrator as well as a pastor and that all staff have job descriptions and all attend weekly staff meetings.*

It is not only the size and funds but the rather informal style of parish that accounts for the absence of staff or staff processes in other parishes. Furthermore, it is clear that different people typically have different hopes or expectations regarding the style of relating. We will look at job descriptions and contracts; performance evaluation and affirmation; organized staff interaction (staff meetings and the like); communication and decision making as components of these relationships.

Job Descriptions and Contracts

Regarding job descriptions and contracts, there are some evident patterns across parishes, though this must be seen still within the general context of the uniqueness of parishes. Actually, given the more "communal" than "organizational" style of parish life, it is a tribute to the care of so many pastors and parish ministers that the majority of parish ministers have job descriptions--almost three-quarters do,[28] about equally among religious and laity. As might be expected, an even higher percentage of the full-time ministers are working with such a description, but still the majority of part-timers have one as well. The ministers least likely to have a description are the general pastoral ministers (only slightly more than a quarter of them do, which is not surprising since they are by definition generalists) and the musicians, whose responsibilities are usually quite clear and limited.[29]

We should not be naive about these job descriptions: the actual responsibilities ministers have often--usually?--varied from those spelled out. Nonetheless, this care in providing job descriptions is remarkable. Furthermore, two-thirds of those with a job description helped to write it. They helped to shape their responsibilities. In this context, we should also point out that the vast majority of parish ministers (more than nine out of ten) reported having "sufficient authority to carry out [their] responsibilities."

Some national organizations related to various ministries have produced guidelines for their constituents' positions: a combination of proposed standards for the ministry, job descriptions, policies affecting the ministries, and salary scales. Examples are the National Conference of Catholic Youth Ministers, the National Association of Pastoral Musicians,[30] and the National Conference of Diocesan Directors of Religious Education, and the National Association of Parish Coordinators/Directors of Religious Education of NCEA.[31] Some dioceses have also promoted job descriptions and guidelines.

Before moving on, we should indicate that at this point we do not want to presume that the job description approach is the best for all parish ministry. The use of job descriptions belongs more to a bureaucratic culture than to a professional one and, given our earlier concern that ministry not be force-fit into a category that does not respect its uniqueness, we feel that there should be more discussion about the roles for which job descriptions are appropriate. Included in this discussion is whether the job description approach harmonizes well with the desire to talk more about vocation than about job when it comes to ministry.[32]

Contracts are another matter and there is less agreement about the value of contracts in these small parish staffs. No less an expert on organizations than Peter Drucker questions the value of contracts for small staffs because small groups need to be more flexible in their arrangements than a contract sometimes allows for. Similarly, the well-respected National Association of Church Personnel Administrators questions the utility of contracts in such situations. Nonetheless, more than half the parish ministers have contracts. It appears that some of the contracts were drawn because religious orders required them for their members, which may account for the fact that religious parish ministers are far more likely than the lay ministers to have contracts. Sometimes diocesan offices required them. Furthermore, contracts seem more frequent among certain ministries: youth ministers are the most likely to have contracts, followed by religious education directors and especially the religious in religious education positions (77 percent).

Yet, the use of job descriptions and contracts can vary not only from parish to parish but within the same parish as well. *In one parish a sister has no job description but has a contract; a lay director of religious education has no contract but a job description; another lay person responsible for liturgy coordination has no job description but a contract.*

Performance Evaluations and Affirmation

Performance evaluations are infrequent: about one in three ministers experience this. Furthermore, of those working full-time, fewer religious than lay people report having regular evaluations and, among the lay people, those in religious education are the least frequently evaluated--for reasons that escape us. Not surprisingly, fewer part-timers undergo evaluation than full-time ministers.

There is not much of a tradition of evaluation in the church (except increasingly of speakers at conferences and conventions). It is the rare diocese that, like the Archdiocese of New York, has instituted evaluations of pastors. Although many ministers speak of support from their pastors, we have seen that many pastors seem reluctant to engage in the very personal and direct communication required by evaluations. Another skill necessary for performance evaluation and one that pastors and pastoral ministers alike indicate is not their strongest suit is that of managing conflict, not meaning here any confrontation, but simply the ability to criticize or say unpleasant things to one another. *Yet, in one parish--exceptional to be sure--everyone is evaluated; the pastor is evaluated by a group of parishioners randomly chosen through a computer program, and their evaluation is published in the parish bulletin. Another exceptional approach to evaluation occurs in one midwest parish: each member of the staff meets with each other member to receive an individual evaluation and then reports to the group as a whole what s/he has learned from the evaluations.*

Another form of "evaluation" is ongoing "affirmation." This is the kind of "feedback" that many ministers are looking for and that gives them assurance that their work is valuable and appreciated. There are some indications from the data and from the site visits that pastors are not always generous with such comments.

Organized Staff Interaction

Many larger staffs--and some smaller ones--seem to have two staffs, an insider group and a somewhat larger group not privy to some of the decision making. The members of the insider or core group can vary: sometimes they are the general pastoral ministers who then relate to those whose work is specialized and/or part-time. Yet, in other staffs, the core group is rather personally chosen by the pastor, including perhaps one of the pastoral ministers and a person who serves as parish administrator or manager.

STAFF ACTIVITIES:
PRACTICES DEEMED IMPORTANT VS. PRACTICES INSTITUTED
(percent)

PRACTICE	Feel Important:		Actually Have:	
	Parish Minister	Pastor	Parish Minister	Pastor
Staff meeting	84.6	71.5	86.7	92.2
Staff prayer (over and above meetings)	72.6	43.2	45.5	59.0
Socializing with staff (outside work)	47.7	33.2	84.8	86.7
Staff work retreats (overnights/full days)	58.6	29.8	37.1	32.0
Staff spiritual days of recollection or retreats	63.8	31.6	36.8	34.5

A few staffs work hard at developing extensive and personal relationships by spending time together not only at work-related staff meetings, but also in regular prayer and "faith sharing," as well as in some socializing. A very few devote part of their meeting time to shared learning of something of value to all of them--perhaps an article they have all read in advance. What those involved want as part of staff relationships varies. Most of the parish ministers (85 percent) want regular staff meetings, but apparently about a fifth of these do not get what they want, for although 87 percent have them, fewer than 60 percent have them regularly. The pastors' preferences lie somewhere between what their ministers want and what they all get; 72 percent of pastors want staff meetings. Beyond these work meetings or as a part of them, almost three quarters of the parish ministers also want time for shared prayer among the staff, but much fewer than half the pastors (43 percent) express this desire, and it is largely where they do that the practice is adopted. Six out of ten of the ministers would also like to have "work retreats" where they could do some general planning and about two-thirds of them would also like to have staff "spiritual days." But only three out of ten pastors see the benefit of these and, with some exceptions, it is only where they do that these times are set aside. Finally, when it comes to socializing among staff, about half of all the ministers--but this is significantly more true among the women religious--see this as a desirable aspect of staff relationships, while only a third of the pastors desire it. In this area, however, the pastors and lay people seem willing to go along with the sisters, for they all report more socializing than all but the sisters want.

There is a real pull here, which is probably inevitable in women-men working groups, especially where sisters who come from a community experience are involved. It is the extent to which the working relationships will be both personal and spiritual relationships. The priests' spiritual practices tend to remain a little more "official" (Mass, liturgy of the hours, and official prayers) and a little less "personally chosen" (Scripture, meditation, devotions, and other forms of prayer) than the sister's. They are more like the lay people's spirituality except for the liturgy of the hours. The sisters are more likely to see staff relationships as personal and spiritual relationships than the priests are. This can be a source of disappointment for the sisters, a challenge for the priests.

It is not surprising that the part-time ministers, who are also more often lay than religious, are less interested in giving time to all these structured gatherings, though a significant number are.

Communication, Decision Making and Collaboration

Communication is at the heart of collaboration.[33] How do the partners in parish ministry see their communication? How do they see that decisions are made?

We have noted that more than four out of five parish ministers reported that they feel free to discuss any difficulties they have with their "supervisor," who is ordinarily the pastor. Regarding communication, a little more than a third (36.4 percent) say that there is "full and open communication among all staff members;" 46.2 percent say the communication is largely of each minister with the pastor and that they both try to keep this communication going; 14.5 percent say that "communication among members of the staff is very limited." Beyond this the parish ministers' perception of the situation is that two-thirds of them feel that the staff cooperate and keep each other informed while each is basically responsible for her or his work and another tenth say they go beyond this and essentially work together on all ministries. Only 22 percent say that they just do their own work without much interaction.

Finally, when it comes to decision making, their situation lines up as the table on the following page displays (arranged in order from the most fully to least collaborative approach). In reading these statistics, please note that there is only one parish minister working with the pastor in 40 percent of these parishes. Consequently, in many cases, choice number three is essentially the same as choice number two. We might then conclude that staff decision making is rather collaborative in more than half these situations. As a matter of fact, 70.4 percent of the parish ministers share in decision-making at least with the pastor, if not with each other. In 5.2 percent of situations they act independently, and in 16.8 percent the pastor restricts decision-making to himself.

DECISION-MAKING STYLES
(percent)

The pastoral members of the staff make most major decisions together with the parish council	20.8
The pastoral members of the staff make most major decisions jointly	12.0
Each makes decisions in her/his area of parish life with the pastor	37.6
Each makes decisions in her/his area of parish life independently	5.2
The pastor makes most major decisions	16.8
Some other method	7.6

How collaborative are the staff relationships? If communication, cooperation, and decision making are part of collaboration, we might conclude that in about three-quarters of the parishes the staff work rather collaboratively. Interestingly enough, when the pastors (with parish staffs) were given a scale on which to place their measure of how "collaborative" vs. "independent" they thought the staff was, only 35 percent chose collaborative (1, 2, or 3 on the ten point scale) while 12 percent found "independent" a better description; the rest put their relationships somewhere between the two styles.

We have seen that the relationships are a combination of what people want, what their own personal practices are, and what structures are established. They also depend on certain relational skills. If it is desirable to foster even more collaborative, to say nothing of more communal, relationships all these contributing factors will have to be considered.

Typical among the satisfactory arrangements are the staffs that relate easily and comfortably, have periodic staff meetings, but essentially work on their own and have modest expectations of a social or spiritual community from serving on the staff. Among these, the pastor most often chairs the staff meetings in however formal or informal a manner, but some deliberately stress shared responsibility by rotating the chairing of the staff meetings. A couple of observer descriptions may be useful:

The staff meets formally every three weeks. At these meetings each person brings issues to the staff for consideration. The pastor initiates many items for the agenda. Informal meetings occur in the interim. With respect to staff evaluations, the pastor noted "the Principal/DRE is evaluated by myself and the school board. Since this was the pastoral associate's first year, I asked her to do a self-evaluation and then the DRE and I reflected with her on the evaluation." From all that I could observe the staff seems to function well and healthily.

They are mature people who have been tempered by life. They seem very clear in what they want in a staff and in a minister. The leadership of the pastor and the quality of the staff enable them to achieve these goals.

Or another:

The pastoral staff [pastor, associate, two lay ministers, and a business manager] seem to relate to each other on a friendly basis, but each operates quite independently of the other. Although Monsignor _____ describes their operating style as a team approach, they do not make decisions together about their respective ministries, nor do they set directions for the parish as a whole. They do not have formal or informal meetings as an entire staff. If meetings are held with individual staff members, these are usually unstructured "pop-in" meetings. Each person keeps Msgr. _____ informed about his or her ministry, but does not necessarily inform the others or seek others' advice about directions or problems in their ministries. The staff does not socialize except on special occasions: according to Msgr._____ those occasions are Secretaries' Day, Christmas and birthdays. One morning I was in the rectory, some members of the pastoral staff were having coffee together in the kitchen and engaging in friendly banter. The pastoral staff never prays together. For the most part, most seem to respect each other.

Or one more:

Each of the ministers [the pastor, an associate pastor, a deacon, a director of religious education, and a youth minister of the same order as the pastor] has a specific area of responsibility but none have job descriptions, nor is there a formal evaluation process in place. Each staff person is ultimately accountable to the pastor. The staff tries to meet on a regular basis, but this often doesn't work out because of time crunches, and the youth minister in fact hates meetings. Staff meetings tend to be roundtable discussion centering on the activities of each staff person; plans and goals for the entire parish are also discussed during the meetings, but decisions tend to be made informally. Father _____ feels that one of the big weaknesses of the pastoral staff is that they need more staff meetings which focus on the direction of the parish. He would like the staff to function as a parish team. According to _____, the DRE, they don't function that way. They still operate as individuals, and this creates "great gaps of information." ...They have sought assistance from [a diocesan agency] to help in their team-building effort. They found this to be moderately helpful, but believe they still have a long way to go.

A few of the parishes have created elaborate charts or diagrams to spell out the relationships between the staff, parish councils, and parishioners. Working in a less articulated structure but in clearly cooperative staff relationships where each nonetheless has a specific job description, one midwest female general pastoral minister declared: *"The whole staff is in collaboration. We all care for everybody." Another type is a series of overlapping relationships perhaps best illustrated by a parish with single priests, a married priest (former Episcopalian), a single lay woman, a married lay man, and a sister. The sister helps the pastor relate to the other staff members. The married lay man who is full-time seems to find considerable peer support from the married priest, while the married priest and one single priest pray the liturgy of the hours together most mornings and, in the process, discuss some ministry concerns. The married lay man and the sister, because both are full-time pastoral ministers and occupy offices in the same building, separate from the rectory where the priests have their offices, also collaborate and find peer support in one another. As a group they do have staff meetings which are rather loosely run by the pastor, but at which everyone seems free to voice their concerns and opinions.*

Given the almost idiosyncratic composition of each pastoral minister's job and the similarly idiosyncratic composition of each parish staff, to say nothing of the shift in expectations among pastoral ministers regarding the kind of relationships that should prevail among parish staffs, it is not surprising that expectations are not always symmetrical or that conflicts and disappointments arise. Neither is it surprising that the structuring of relationships is not always based on the positions people occupy. It can be influenced by both personal factors and the relative competence of the various ministers, especially in the eyes of the pastor. Where people come to parish staffs from an experience of a close working community, such as some sisters have enjoyed and others have had in either charismatic or Catholic Worker or other communities, they can easily be disappointed in the less extensive and intensive community of a parish staff. One still hears frequently about a "team" approach to staff relationships, but there may be more realism about what this approach means and about the organized procedures required to make the team effective in their ministry and supportive of one another. One staff acknowledged that a team approach is "inefficient, requires considerable communication, and needs time to reach consensus." At the same time, this approach offers "companionship, sharing, vitality, creativity, use of gifts."

VII: Contributions to Parish Ministry

T he contributions the lay/religious ministers make to parish life depend on their own lives and experience as religious or lay, as married or single, as well as on the positions they occupy in the parish, and the perceptions of their contributions in the eyes of the pastors and parishioners. Some of these contributions have to do with their sensibilities, such as regarding the concerns of women or men or family life, which can affect all the works they do. Some of their influence lies in enabling parishioners to deepen their faith and their commitment to its consequences, as well as to get involved or deepen their involvement in parish concerns and ministries. *As one parishioner reported about a lay woman minister: "M. has turned me on to the church, to theology and liturgy. She does this in a quiet and non-threatening way. She can make virtue seem cozy. She has a gift of being able to attract new people."*

The contribution can also come from the special expertise lay ministers bring to religious education, liturgy, or music. It may be their ability to relate to a particular group in the parish, such as the youth. Still, according to the testimony of pastors and parishioners, other contributions derive as much from the lay minister's personality and native ability to relate to people as from their vocational status, training, ministry, or other aspect of parish ministry. Thus, some are gifted with particular compassion and understanding which encourage parishioners to turn to them in times of need and to find in them the support that is encouraging.

It is in such complex terms that the pastoral ministers themselves, the pastors, and the parishioners almost always talk about their contribution to the community and mission of the parish.

It is in the context of these measures, therefore, that our discussion of "contribution" to parish life in this section amounts to a discussion of a key variable of this study, namely the "effectiveness" of the parish ministers. Effectiveness is not easy to measure, in part because the church rarely spells out measures of effectiveness.[34] Nor do church leaders embrace common standards for parish life. There are very valuable lists of a pastor's responsibilities in Canons 528 and 529 and in other parts of the Code of Canon Law. The statement published by the Committee on the Parish of the National Conference of Catholic Bishops proposes a vision of what a good parish might look like.[35] But neither the actions required nor the results expected have become common currency in church life. Nor are these or any other statements the basis for any widespread practice of evaluating parishes, pastors, or any other parish ministers.

The absence of measures or standards of effectiveness can even be a matter of principle for those who fear that emphasis on effectiveness could undercut the priority of **authenticity** in ministry. For to remain "authentic" in these terms means to be faithful to church teaching and discipline, whatever the outcome for the individual minister or for the church, whatever the effects. In the extreme, both the parish minister and the parish may suffer for preaching and acting in accordance with the authentic message of the church by being dismissed as irrelevant to contemporary life, which can be more significant than the perverted tribute martyrdom represents.

Another argument against discussing effectiveness stresses that the human "proposes and God disposes"--that it is God who works through the minister and often through the weaknesses of the individual. The minister is an instrument whose inadequacies do not limit God's action.

Effectiveness is nonetheless not contrary to authenticity and some measures are inevitably, if unprofessedly, used. Of course, what is effective in one situation may not be effective in another. Yet without discussing effectiveness any discussion of accountability becomes severely restricted to protection against violations of orthodoxy or orthopraxy. Accountability becomes only a matter of "damage limitation." To state this does not make it any easier to agree about effectiveness, for one is still left with the problem of criteria. What criteria are to be used? We discussed this problem at length with our advisory committee and have tackled the issue in a variety of ways.

First, we have asked the parish ministers themselves and their counterparts--the pastors, other ordained members of the parish staffs, and parishioners--what contribution, if any, they have made to a wide range of parish concerns. Regarding the following list of concerns, we asked if they thought the ministers' own ministry has:

> Added considerably
> [Made] Some improvement
> Continued what was there
> Made it worse

The possible contributions were (with admittedly mixed syntax):

1. Deepening parish spirituality
2. Ability to reach more parishioners
3. Competency in more areas/skills
4. Enabling parishioners to feel at home in the parish

5. Improvement of liturgy/worship
6. Improvement of religious education
7. Pastoral care to those with various needs
8. Counselling
9. Spirit of community
10. Outreach to wider community concerns
11. Sensitivity to family concerns
12. Sensitivity to women's concerns
13. Sensitivity to men's concerns
14. Sensitivity to social justice concerns
15. Understanding of lay concerns
16. Involvement of women
17. Involvement of men
18. Involvement of elderly
19. Involvement of youth
20. Management of parish resources
21. Communication within the parish
22. General strengthening of parish life
23. Staff collaboration
24. Parish vision and sense of mission
25. Planning

As the reader can see, the list includes parish activities (worship, religious education, etc.), groups or constituencies in the parish (women, men, elderly, youth) concerning whom we ask about sensitivity to their concerns and involving them in the parish, processes of parish life (planning, communication, collaboration), and two very general categories--the "vision and sense of mission" that set priorities for a parish, and "general strengthening of parish life." We also asked whether the addition was of some skill that would otherwise be lacking and/or simply that more persons on staff can reach more parishioners.

A second measure of effectiveness was tapped in the survey section that asks the ministers about skills or kinds of activity (e.g., teaching, organizing): are these activities part of their work? do they feel adequately prepared to perform them? and do they perform them well or not?

Our third approach to the question of effectiveness had to do with others' satisfaction with the ministers' performance. While it is true that parishioner satisfaction or the popularity of a minister is not necessarily a reliable measure of effectiveness (here is where certain standards of authenticity, theology, and taste are important), nonetheless, active parishioners can be good judges of the impact (a kind of effectiveness) of those ministering to them. This is especially true if one determines that an important "effect" of good ministry is establishing a good relationship with the parishioners as a condition for engaging them more fully in the community and ministry of discipleship.

Parishioners' views of the contributions that lay ministers make to parish life depend, in part, on how much the parishioner knows about the working of the parish. Some ministers' work is visible only to those who are very active in parish organizations and events; others find themselves in the public eye at liturgies and in ministries that bring them into contact with many adults and their contribution is more evident and appreciated. Because of the problem of the observability of individual ministers' performance, we chose to solicit the opinions not of a random sample of parishioners but of an informed group, members of parish councils or parishioners who are otherwise active enough to be in a position to offer a useful critique. Half the parishioners consulted had been parishioners in the parish 17 years or longer, half for a shorter time, and 42 percent were members of parish pastoral councils and 21 percent members of parish finance councils.

A good statement of what parishioners appreciate and how their views may be affected by how well they understand and observe the parish minister's role comes from this interview with parishioners in a farm-belt parish:

In general the parishioners have been satisfied with the work of the pastoral associate. In particular, they feel that Sister L_____ has done a lot in the two communities [a parish and mission]. She does quite a bit of one-on-one ministry and has contributed to developing the liturgical sense of the parishioners. They felt that she put her heart and soul into her ministry. She has always tried to get parishioners involved and to bring them along. They admitted that others in the parish questioned her role. To a large extent, these people mistakenly thought she was hired to teach religion, though she was not. They questioned her being paid $2,400 annually [!]. Her part-time status probably contributed to this confusion.

In short, in this section we are treating the activities of the parish ministers, their influence on the parishioners and the ministries of the parish, and how well-satisfied the parishioners are with the ministers. We are looking at these factors through the eyes of the ministers themselves, the pastors, the other ordained ministers, and active parishioners.

Contribution to Parishioners and Ministries

The most important statement to make is that the vast majority of all consulted agree that the lay and religious parish ministers make a significant contribution to parish life. A word about the measures we provided and, therefore, that they used. As we mentioned, the choices were:" Added considerably," "Some improvement," "Continued what was there," and "Made it worse." Of course, even to continue what was there may well mean to serve quite adequately. Very few of any group judged that these parish ministers had worsened any of these aspects of parish life. The only disagreement about the level of their contribution is that the pastors tend to rate the parish ministers' contributions higher than do the ministers themselves and than do the parishioners; the parish ministers and parishioners tend to see things the same way. In thirteen of the twenty-five areas of impact we listed above, four out of five pastors found that the parish ministers "added considerably" or at least "made some improvement." And in all but two of the other categories, about two-thirds or more felt the same way. We will discuss the specifics in a moment. Where four-fifths of the pastors speak of a contribution, about three-quarters of the parishioners and parish ministers make the same judgment.

The table on the following page indicates the percentage of each group of respondents who think the lay ministers "added considerably" or made "some improvement." The items with asterisks are those where the largest percentage of each group thinks the parish ministers "added considerably" to the life of the parish.

Two factors may account for the higher estimation by pastors than by the ministers themselves. First, we are often our own worst judges. Secondly, the pastors are making judgments about the effects of all the ministers together, while each parish minister is judging only her or his own performance. Thus, pastors may say that lay and religious parish ministers have improved the parish's religious education, while the individual parish minister who has no responsibility for religious education would not claim any contribution to that ministry.

Clearly, there is broad agreement that the greatest impact has been made in the parish's ability simply to reach more people, the enabling of parishioners to feel at home in the parish, and religious education.[36] The parish ministers and the pastors also agree that the parish ministers bring additional skills to the ministry of the parish. Another angle of vision on the same items is that three-quarters of the parish ministers, pastors, and parishioners agree that the parish ministers make a contribution to:

> Deepening parish spirituality
> Ability to reach more parishioners
> Competency in more areas/skills
> Enabling parishioners to feel at home
> Improvement of religious education
> Spirit of community
> General strengthening of parish life

WHAT LAY/RELIGIOUS MINISTRY ADDS TO PARISH LIFE:
(percent who answered either "Some Improvement" or "Added Considerably")

ADDITIONS TO PARISH LIFE	- - - - - - - - - - - Views of - - - - - - - - - - -			
	Parish Minister	Pastor	Parishioners	Other Staff
Deepening parish spirituality	76.4	86.5	78.8	76.8
Ability to reach more parishioners	83.8*	89.6*	81.8*	85.3
Competency in more areas/skills	76.9*	85.1*	74.9	74.2
Enabling parishioners to feel at home	78.8*	86.0*	77.9*	77.7*
Improvement of liturgy/worship	61.6	81.8	80.3	72.0
Improvement of religious education	70.0*	85.3*	78.5*	83.8*
Pastoral care to various needs	54.1	82.2	75.8	81.2*
Counselling	39.1	53.5	54.8	46.5
Spirit of community	75.4	84.5	76.6	73.9
Outreach to wider community concerns	60.9	73.9	68.5	69.7
Sensitivity to family needs	68.6	80.0	67.6*	74.4
Sensitivity to women's concerns	55.4	76.2	55.7	64.1
Sensitivity to men's concerns	35.8	50.6	46.1	46.8
Sensitivity to social justice concerns	57.6	63.5	61.8	59.1
Understanding of lay concerns	64.3	74.7	66.2	68.2
Involvement of women	67.3	82.8	80.0	79.4*
Involvement of men	52.6	67.6	68.3	64.7
Involvement of elderly	41.5	64.1	57.5	61.7
Involvement of youth	60.7	67.0	68.5	63.3
Management of parish resources	44.5	68.2	71.5	58.2
Communication within the parish	74.4	83.1	75.3	68.5
General strength of parish life	74.9	89.4	79.7	77.4
Staff collaboration	67.1	81.4	71.2	64.4
Parish vision and sense of mission	68.4	81.1	76.4	66.2
Planning	72.9	81.4	78.6	63.2

* Items with highest percent of those who think L/RM made the greatest impact, that is, "added considerably."

With but a hair's measure less confidence among the parish ministers themselves, there is broad agreement of the ministers' contribution to:

> Communication within the parish
> Planning

The other parish ministers, the ordained parochial vicars and deacons, where these exist, tend to be more positive in almost all areas than the parish ministers themselves and just slightly less positive than the parishioners.

The ability of the ministers to relate to various people in the parishes was underscored in our site visits. Many parishioners commented that the women in ministry both offered more understanding of and sensitivity to women's concerns than the priest could, and provided a "role model" of a woman in a spiritual leadership position. *A Hispanic woman minister gave evidence of identifying especially well with the Hispanic culture and Hispanic women's concerns in the southwest parish where she serves. Still another black woman's complex background and experience have made an important contribution to her ministry. The observer's report spells this out at some length:*

> *A. has an undergraduate degree in social work. She worked for ten years as a child protection worker and continues to use the skills gained there in counselling parishioners. She specialized with victims of sexual abuse, and counsels children in the school and parish abused sexually.*

> *She has a master's degree in pastoral ministry....She draws heavily on the knowledge gained through the...program and still consults with several of her professors. She is just completing a master's in theology from the Institute for Black Catholic studies at Xavier University in New Orleans....This program has helped her to understand herself and her parish as rooted in the black social and religious experience,.....A.'s own religious and life experiences have influenced her greatly in her ministry--in fact, they led her into ministry. She said that when she was pregnant with her first child she was experiencing a very hard time. "I had a religious experience then and met God in grace. I became a lector so that I could share the Good News with others." This led to other ministries and eventually to her present position in the parish.*

As might be expected, parish ministers do not all have the same impact in all areas. The most obvious reason for differences lies in their different responsibilities, which should be noted. However, here we can only report the parish ministers' own views because it was not feasible to track the views of the pastors, parochial vicars, and parishioners regarding each parish minister.

To state the most obvious distinction: 61 percent of the religious educators think that they have added considerably to the parishes' religious education programs. In a similar vein, 71 percent of the youth ministers feel confident that they have made a real difference in youth ministry. The areas where the general parish ministers feel they have made the greatest contribution (a third or more think they have "added considerably") are those of inclusiveness or general participation of the parishioners: ability to reach more parishioners (48 percent), pastoral care to those with various needs (48 percent), enabling the parishioners to feel at home in the parish (48 percent), improving the spirit of community in the parish (41 percent), strengthening parish life (39 percent), and involvement of women (39 percent), but also of the religious education program (35 percent). By definition, the generalists have no single area where the great majority of them claim considerable impact--their role varies with the parish, their impact is spread among a number of areas of parish life. To go back to the religious educators for a moment, the aspects of parish life which they feel they have most affected are the addition to the parish staff of their competency as religious educators and the various ways of reaching more parishioners and making them feel at home in their parish.

We also need to note where the parish ministers feel they have the least influence, feelings generally shared by the others in the parish. All agree that the parish ministers are least successful in their sensitivity to men's concerns--though they do somewhat better involving men in the activity of the parish, better even than involving the elderly. This is even true among the youth ministers, half of whom are men--involvement of men and sensitivity to men's concerns are where they feel they have the least impact. This is a complex matter. First, it is true that, in general, church life attracts more women than men and these ministers are in effect saying that they don't do much to change that. Second, if one asks oneself what are "men's concerns"? the answer does not come as easily to mind as what have been called women's concerns in recent years. Third, to the extent that one talks about job-related concerns as a possible point of contact, which of course are more and more shared by women, the "Chicago Declaration" and the National Center for the Laity have indeed lamented the failure of parish life to assist parishioners with the challenge of being Christians "in the marketplace."

Another area where all agree that the parish ministers have very little impact is "counselling." When we consider their training, we will see that they feel little prepared for this kind of ministry, but we should also note that a significant minority regard this as part of their responsibility.

Few of the parish ministers think they have much of an impact on the elderly, though everyone else gives them more credit for influence, but again this is not an area for which many of them were hired.

To return to the beginning of this section, the parish ministers are recognized by all to make a real contribution to parish life. Are there areas where they seem to detract from parish life? Only a few of the almost one thousand in our sample feel this is true in each area, but the numbers are so small they are hardly worth considering.

Skills and Performance

We have earlier discussed how well prepared the parish ministers are regarding the knowledge and skills required for their work. What now about their exercise of these skills, whatever their preparation? The following indicates their own perception of their level of performance; we repeat their perceptions of their preparation for comparative purposes.

Where are the greatest shortcomings among the parish ministers, the skills they feel called upon to exercise but don't feel they do well at? The biggest gaps between it's "part of my work" and I "perform well" were in: managing conflict (two-thirds feel it's part of their work and only half of these think they do well); motivating involvement (while three-quarters acknowledge this as part of their work almost a quarter of them don't think they measure up); collaborating (four out of five feel they need to do this, but only two-thirds judge their performance as good); supervising others (while slightly over 70 percent feel called upon to do this, less than 60 percent think they do well at it), and public communication--speaking, writing (three-quarters feel called upon to do this and only a little over two-thirds feel they carry it off well).

Do the pastors have the same estimation of the parish ministers' performance in these areas? (We did not include this section in the other survey forms.) In every single area without exception, the pastors have a significantly more positive view of the skills of the parish ministers. The pastors generally share the parish ministers' view that performance falls short of what's needed in managing conflict, but they see much less room for improvement in the other areas where the parish ministers feel inadequate. In short, the pastors register considerable appreciation for the skills of their parish ministers.

PREPARATION AND PERFORMANCE IN SKILLS FOR MINISTRY
Ministers' Views of Themselves
(skills 75 percent or more most commonly need)

SKILL	Adequately Prepared	Perform Well
Communicating one-on-one	76.9	81.2
Planning	72.9	76.7
Building community	68.2	72.9
Organizing projects	66.0	71.7
Collaborating	65.4	67.1
Motivating people to become involved	53.0	59.6
Communicating to public groups	63.6	66.9
Teaching	68.1	69.5

(additional skills 67 percent or more most commonly need)

SKILL	Adequately Prepared	Perform Well
Supervising others	55.4	59.0
Hospitality	61.7	64.3
Leading/co-leading prayer	59.1	62.3
Training	60.0	62.9

Parish Ministers and Parishioners

Of course, the basic object of all pastoral ministry, that of clergy and laity alike, is to enable the parishioners to be all that a parish should be. The ministers are neither to usurp the responsibilities of the parishioners nor are they to turn the parishioners into parish ministers, so preoccupied with the organizations of parish life that they have little time or energy for their own family and other communities or for the mission of the Gospel in the affairs of the world. In fact, the picture that emerges from our study of the relationships between parish ministers and parishioners is a complex one and this may be the best place to discuss it.

First, we have already noted the increasing involvement of parishioners through parish councils and other committees in determining the staff positions to be filled and in the search and screening process of hiring staff.

Second, in some instances, the parish minister is accountable to a council committee or some other group that has responsibility for an area of parish ministry. *In one parish, the council members spoke of the tension that existed between the director of liturgy and music and the liturgy commission of parishioners regarding ultimate authority over the liturgy and indicated that the commission members had finally gotten through to the minister that they were in charge.* We have also found from a content analysis of the job descriptions (accompanying parish minister surveys) that where the parish minister is accountable to a committee or commission of a council rather than to the pastor, there is a tendency for the parish minister to have less authority and for the parishioners to require more approvals for action.

Third, do the parish ministers substitute for the parishioners' own ministry to one another or do the parish ministers enable more parishioners to be involved? We have already discussed this but the matter warrants further comment. There is discussion in the church of the danger that the new lay ministers can add a kind of "staffism" to the already present danger of "clericalism" in parish life, i.e., the tendency to take over responsibility for the life and work of the parish as to usurp the responsibilities of the parishioners themselves. In a few instances, this seems to be true: very competent ministers who provide great service to the parish, but do not encourage parishioners to take on these services and provide ways for them to do so. More typical, however, are the comments from parishioners that the lay ministers helped people to get involved in religious education, youth ministry, liturgy, pastoral care for one another and in other kinds of concerns. *As one parishioner put it, the lay/religious ministers contribute to parishioner involvement in two ways: one is that their caring for others encourages people who can be very much preoccupied with their own concerns also to be concerned about others. Second, lay/religious ministers, simply by providing additional staffing to parish projects, assure people, who want to participate but whose family and other responsibilities must come first, that the parish minister will be ultimately responsible for the work should some family obligation arise.* The new parish ministers, for the most part, seem both convinced about the need to involve parishioners and adept at doing so. Furthermore, the parish ministers and the parishioners largely agree about parishioners' readiness to volunteer, as the table on the following page indicates.

But we looked at this question in another way. While parish ministers get parishioners involved for limited amounts of time as catechists, catechumenate sponsors, participants in youth ministry, as liturgical ministers, choir members, and ministers to the sick and shut-ins, to name a few ways, would more parishioners actually become volunteer staff if the ministers were not hired? We asked the parishes to let us know how much parishioners were actually serving in extensive and responsible ways, giving twenty hours a week or more to the work of the parish. We examined this phenomenon in relation to hired staff and find that there is no clear conclusion: the presence of hired staff is neither negatively nor positively linked with such staffing by parishioners. In no consistent fashion do the hired ministers invite this kind of involvement or discourage it.

WHEN ASKED, DO PARISHIONERS VOLUNTEER?
(percent)

FREQUENCY	Parishioners' View	Parish Ministers' View
Always	14.8	11.1
Usually	49.0	45.7
Sometimes	28.8	34.8
Seldom	7.3	8.1
Never	0.2	0.3

Fourth, what do the parishioners want from these parish ministers? The study offers some interesting insights, related in part to an earlier study by Dean Hoge. We asked the parishioners--remember these are not a sample of all parishioners, but a select group of highly involved and well-informed parishioners--whether they thought the religious and lay parish ministers should do some things currently or formerly restricted to the priests. The results are interesting.

A few words about the table on page 90. First, while the percentage of "No" among the parishioners would be obvious if we simply listed the "Yes" column, we added the "No" to make clear where there was decided opposition, namely regarding weddings and funerals. This confirms the findings of Dean Hoge and his associates that the parishioners want priests at these events.[37]

Second, we included "some lead role at the Eucharist" because some parish ministers have argued the need for a visible role when the parish assembles for worship if they are to be seen by the parishioners in a responsible position. Oddly enough, the parishioners and pastors tend to think this is a good idea, but the majority of parish ministers are not so quick to agree.

But there is a even more curious phenomenon here. For we asked all which of these activities the parish ministers already do. Here we will look only at the parish ministers' and pastors' views, because they should know best the current practices.

WHICH OF THE FOLLOWING DO YOU THINK THE LAY/RELIGIOUS MINISTERS OUGHT TO BE ABLE TO DO OR SHARE IN DOING?
(percent)

ACTIVITY	Parishioners' Opinion		Parish Ministers' Opinion	Pastors' Opinion
	Yes	No	Yes	Yes
Preside at weddings	33.7	66.3	6.9	31.4
Do marriage preparation	86.0	14.0	19.0	77.5
Conduct wake services	61.4	38.6	23.9	70.2
Have some lead role at the Eucharist	73.0	27.0	39.6	70.2
Control some budget	84.4	15.6	52.7	76.9
Hire staff	60.3	39.7	30.9	49.2
Take part in parish council meetings	97.7	2.3	60.7	84.1
Relate directly to diocesan offices	81.4	18.6	62.6	81.8
Visit parish homes	96.4	3.6	48.6	85.3
Take part in work of parish school	95.4	4.6	28.3	57.8
Lead prayer services	93.7	6.3	64.1	88.8
Preach	55.6	44.4	26.5	46.5
Preside at funeral services	36.6	63.4	14.3	44.5

The table on page 91 indicates that many parish ministers are already doing what people want them to do, but that parishioners are open to much more involvement by these parish ministers. Again, the higher percentages among pastors can be accounted for by the fact that they are commenting on all the ministers as a group; if some do the activity and some do not, still he will say yes. There may well be some ambiguity in the wording of the items, which allows more to claim that activity than actually do what we intended. Nonetheless, the wording is not very obscure and probably does tap more involvement in certain activities than we had realized.

To complete this section, it does appear that all agree the parish ministers are making a significant contribution and that, in the eyes of both the parishioners and pastors, they should be invited to share even more fully in the work of the parish.

There are areas where these ministers are not notably successful but they are probably areas where the parish as a whole needs improvement. We think of the relationships of men to parish life and the difficulties of collaborating, motivating people to become involved, and managing the inevitable conflicts that arise in parishes.

WHICH OF THESE ACTIVITIES DO PARISH MINISTERS NOW DO?
(percent responding "yes")

ACTIVITY	Views of	
	Parish Ministers	Pastors
Preside at weddings	2.7	13.1
Do marriage preparation	13.4	46.3
Conduct wake services	14.2	42.5
Have some lead role at the Eucharist	37.7	58.6
Control some budget	47.7	67.8
Hire staff	26.3	40.0
Take part in parish council meetings	53.9	74.3
Relate directly to diocesan offices	53.9	81.8
Visit parish homes	45.7	69.8
Take part in work of parish school	28.1	51.2
Lead prayer services	64.8	82.4
Preach	14.3	28.8
Preside at funeral services	8.1	19.2

*   *   *

To conclude this section, the parish ministers have made an enormous contribution to parish life, by their abilities as well as their numbers. In the eyes of all involved they have enhanced parish life in almost all respects. The parishioners, for the most part, would look to them for even more broader involvement in parish life, though the particular charism and formation for priesthood remains of great importance for all. There are areas, such as counselling, where better preparation might make for better ministry, and the ministers could use better developed skills for supervision, training and others aspects of their ministry. It will also become important to achieve greater clarity about the accountability of the ministers: what role if any is appropriate for parish councils and committees? It will also be important to recognize the variety of skills involved in the various ministry positions and to encourage these in formation and continuing education programs.

VIII: Working Conditions

Small and family businesses are notorious for their difficult working conditions: long hours, low salaries, frequent lack of health and other benefits, tight working spaces, and expectations that the personal commitments of all involved will make these difficult conditions at least tolerable. Something of this shows up in the parishes. The tendency to hire on a part-time basis women parishioners for whom this is their first employment outside the home since their first child and/or whose husband's occupation provides the main family support and health insurance leads to a lean approach to ministry compensation. At best, even when the parish is hiring a professional minister on a full-time basis, the compensation may well be just but will never be very great. Nor do the lay ministers expect to get rich working in ministry: to a person, they profess that, while they need income adequate to their needs, they keep their needs as modest as possible and regard the privilege of ministry as far more important than the income they receive. One married man who left his position as principal in a public school to accept the pastor's invitation to take the combined position of parochial school teacher and DRE (he later became the parish school principal) took a sharp cut in salary:

> *I did this only after long consideration and with the support of my wife. Going to Catholic school meant I would take a $7,000 cut in salary. We had two children and that was not an easy decision for me. Yet I felt the Lord was calling me. Without the support and encouragement of my wife I couldn't have done this.*

In fact, the work condition that is the most troublesome is the salary and fringe benefits. This is especially true for the lay persons and seems most keenly felt by women who are expecting to support themselves and their families or young men in youth ministry who are looking ahead to the same responsibilities. One person put the concern this way:

> *"Men are forced to leave ministry if they intend to marry and have a family. Women stay, if it's a second income. Salary is simply prohibitive to long-term ministry. Add to this that benefits are few, there is little or no opportunity for advancement and no long-term jobs and it becomes very difficult for lay people to remain in ministry.*

How much are they paid? The following table indicates for each full-time (35 hours or more) ministry position the average hours worked, salary, and total costs (salary plus benefits and extras), as well as the hourly cost (salary and extras divided by hours).

WORKING HOURS AND COMPENSATION
Full-time Ministers
(percent)

POSITION	Yearly Salary	Yearly Total	Hours Per	Hourly Wage
General Minister	$15,130	$19,981	44.6	$8.70
Religious Educator	$15,928	$20,411	43.2	$9.60
Liturgist	$19,735	$25,453	42.4	$11.77
Music Minister	$17,490	$21,458	42.1	$9.37
Youth Minister	$17,518	$22,410	41.2	$10.24
Other	$12,973	$18,351	46.8	$8.03

Actually the part-timers are paid at least comparably with, and the part-time music ministers are paid significantly better than, their full-time colleagues: they receive an average of $17.99 an hour compared with the $9.37 of the full-timers.

As context for the remarks from the site visits, what do the ministers think of their compensation according to the survey? Obviously we need to consider the laity and religious separately. First, the lay parish ministers. When it comes to meeting one's "personal needs," 45 percent of the lay parish ministers (part-time and full-time) think the salary is excellent (6 percent) or good (39 percent). Forty-two percent regard it as "fair" and only 13 percent say poor. When one adds in family needs, the picture shifts somewhat, but not so dramatically--slightly fewer wind up in the excellent, good, and fair categories (5, 35, and 40 percent, respectively), and now 20 percent regard the salary as poor. Only 18 percent regard the salary as poor when it is compared to other workers in the area. Good enough to keep them working in the church? Perhaps not. Almost three out of five (59 percent) think that there may come a time that they will no longer be able to afford to keep working in the church. This is especially true among the youth ministers (73 percent) and liturgists (63 percent) and least a problem for the general pastoral ministers. Furthermore, a fifth of all the parish ministers (lay and religious, part-time and full-time) target salary as the primary factor needing improvement in the future.

An increasing number of women religious are also indicating a difficulty with their stipends, rarely because of their own needs, though this may be a problem as well, but mostly because of the needs of their congregations. While 94 percent of the religious found that the salary or stipend meets their personal needs, at least minimally, 5 percent fewer find it meets their congregation's needs and 29 percent say that there may come a time when they will no longer be able to afford to work in the **church**, not just the parish, but the church!

While some dioceses have salary and stipend guidelines, especially regarding school teachers and religious education directors (and in New England, the New England Religious Education Directors Association has drawn up salary guidelines for the dioceses of the region) the compensation situation for the most part reflects the autonomy of the parishes and their relative financial resources as well as the diverse attitudes and approaches of pastors to such employment matters. Even where there are diocesan guidelines, these are often established without pastor participation in the process and some pastors can be unaware of them.

One report:

Both persons [paid ministers] said that if one wanted to make this a long-time career, the issue of salary would have to be addressed. One minister noted "I feel called to minister in the church. However a major obstacle to a lifetime career is salary. This reality would make it hard for me to live out my call to lay ministry. I would have to deny it. Now I am young and single and can move to another career. But I could never make it with a family. Right now I am living on the edge financially with little medical benefits and no pension. I also got no cost of living raise, so I don't feel appreciated."

The National Association of Church Personnel Administrators (NACPA) has led the way in promoting just salaries and working conditions for those in ministerial positions. As an association of diocesan and religious order personnel directors, NACPA reflects a growing awareness in the church of the need to ensure reasonable salaries, health and other benefits, and pensions. The picture that emerges here is that between 10 and 20 percent of the lay persons and religious have relatively strong complaints about their compensation, about a third or more find the compensation minimally reasonable or "fair," and about four out of ten or more find the compensation good or better than that.

Time Demands

Parish life is inherently demanding. Parish ministry cannot be contained within normal working hours and will always involve evening and weekend hours. The amount of time required and the particular times required will always be in tension with private life. This tension is evident in our reports. Almost every parish report carries a story of a pastoral minister working longer hours than originally bargained for and currently paid for. This is as true for the part-timers, who find themselves working thirty or forty hours though they are paid for only twenty hours, as for full-timers who talk about the many long hours, reaching up to eighty hours in one minister's estimate. Of course, difficulties arise not simply from the number of hours but also because these work hours are often in the evening and on weekends, thus competing with personal life and family or religious community needs. Almost 16 percent of the lay people and 8 percent of the religious experience "a great deal of conflict" between the time demands of their parish work and their own needs, and another 57 percent of the lay people and 49 percent of the religious experience some conflict in this regard. Interestingly enough, there is almost no difference among the lay people between those who are married and those who are single: they experience time conflicts to the same degree (75 percent vs. 72 percent, respectively).

When it comes specifically to the requirements of being at the parish in the evenings or on weekends, almost half the lay people find this difficult and three out of ten religious also find it difficult.

Having said this, it is perhaps encouraging how many do not complain about these hours and are prepared to accept the special demands of parish ministry. Yet, clearly many find the hours difficult, the gap between expectations and compensation rather unjust, and the conflict between ministry demands and personal and family needs stressful. Furthermore, sisters report these conflicts of time as well, though not quite to the same degree as the lay ministers.

Some balance will be required about this if people are to perdure and give evidence of the values they are promoting, namely the values of family life and personal development, while not reducing parish ministry to office hours and limited service.

Of special concern are two positions: the parish life coordinator (the one who "pastors" the parish in the absence of a resident priest) and the youth minister. The very nature of the former position, one that has always required endless hours of the priests who have occupied it, makes it difficult to introduce a clear and reliable schedule, if the coordinator is to ensure the planned ministries and respond to the unpredictable requests for help. The youth minister is subject to the disorder in young people's lives and their expectation that they can get help at any hour of the day. These positions place ministers in jeopardy of "burnout" because they have so little control over their time. It's one thing to expect this kind of availability from celibate ministers (who themselves are introducing more protective measures such as office hours and answering machines), but quite another to expect this from lay ministers, married or single.

Physical Arrangements

A third condition is the work space allotted to each minister. Just as many parishes have only minimally reshaped the space in churches to meet the requirements of reformed liturgy, many parishes have grave difficulty in accommodating the new ministers in existing rectories and other parish buildings. In spite of the often tight working spaces, little meeting space or privacy and other physical constraints on ministry, it is to their credit that the vast majority find their space, its location, and other physical conditions adequate. Actually, the pastors are less sure of this, ten percent fewer of them think the space is good.

When staffs have more than one or two ministers, often they find themselves working in separate buildings. This separation has two consequences: it often indicates which ministry the pastor regards as more important and it makes communication and cooperation more difficult. In addition, since parishes typically have only general support staff mainly accountable to the pastor, even if it is stated that this staff will provide secretarial assistance to the other ministers, the physical separation aggravates the already present reluctance of some support staff to serve any but the priests (and especially to serve the often young lay minister). The effect is that lay people without secretarial skills must provide both the direct ministry and office back-up, again not surprising in small non-profit staffs, but a factor that needs consideration nonetheless.

The current tendency to separate priests' residences, parish offices, and meeting spaces will relieve some of the difficulties. It is not hard to see, however, the new danger of creating a more bureaucratic atmosphere in parish ministry than might have existed when the priest saw people "at home." Procedures for effectiveness and efficiency--secretaries, computers, office hours, answering services and machines, and the very image of offices when one enters some rectories and parish buildings can significantly change the pastor and parish minister relationships with the parishioners, introducing a professional/client or bureaucrat/customer relationship.

All in all, the working conditions on the average are reasonably good, but will require more attention to ensure that these conditions of compensation, time, and physical arrangements are addressed fairly by all parishes and do not depend on the varying abilities of the parishes to work through these matters.

IX: Satisfactions of Parish Ministry

T his study required us to consider not only the ministry lay and religious ministers perform and how well they are prepared to do it and are seen to do it, but also how satisfying this ministry is to the ministers themselves. For their perdurance in the ministry will in part depend on whether they find the work rewarding and feel that their efforts are appreciated by others, the parishioners, pastors, and other parish ministers with whom they minister.

Frankly, we struggled with the proper frame of reference for this aspect of the study. Was it to be a matter of "success" in ministry and the feelings of "achievement" in ministry? To some extent we did measure this by looking at what contribution the ministers think they make to the parish and what contributions others see. For surely what helps people to stay committed to a work, to maintain good "morale," is some sense that their work is effective, has results. Yet, one can feel committed to a work whose results seem elusive simply because the work is important and represents a witness to important values.

Should we measure happiness? There is no easy measure of happiness and no assurance that happiness always accompanies work that is valuable, work with which one is content.

We chose the term satisfaction, not a new term in occupational studies or even in popular discussions. We don't mean self-satisfied, the state of settling into a life and work that provides the least challenge or disturbance. Rather satisfaction in this study denotes the feeling that this is a good work to do, that the conditions are supportive and respectful, that those one wishes to serve feel that they are indeed served, that one's own abilities are being well used in the work. To achieve measures of satisfaction, we decided to approach the question from a great variety of perspectives, some of which we have already reported and will have to resume here. We asked the simple question: is the working situation satisfying or not? Yes or no? But we also asked:

How are the physical work conditions, salary, time demands, space, etc.?

What adjectives best describe the work, terms such as fascinating, routine, boring, good, creative, respected, tiresome, challenging, frustrating?

What are the relationships like with fellow parish ministers and parishioners, and how affirming are these people? Do these meet one's hopes?

What other supports does one have?

We also asked these ministers how long they expected to stay in the ministry of their present parish and of the church and would they encourage others to do what they are doing? We thought these might be the real test: it's one thing to speak well of a work, it's another to encourage others to get into it.

Of course, we also have examined all of these measures of satisfaction against each other to see if they are redundant, and against all sorts of other information about the parish ministers--their age and education, the particular ministries they are performing and the situation in which they perform it--all to see what factors seem most to affect satisfaction and commitment to the future, what factors seem to be associated most with discouragement and doubt about the future. We will see that simple statements are often quite adequate to measure satisfaction and that the contributing factors are not all that obscure.

Probably the most important statement to make in this regard, however, is that the vast majority of these parish ministers find their ministry very satisfying. A few measures quickly tell this story:

Is the ministry satisfying?   Yes - 93.5 percent.
Does it give a sense of accomplishment?   Yes - 92 percent.
Is it spiritually rewarding?   Yes - 91.5 percent.

CHARACTERISTICS OF "WORKING SITUATION"
(percent saying each describes their work)

Positive traits:
Fascinating	63.3
Satisfying	93.5
Good	91.9
Creative	88.1
Respected	86.3
Challenging	94.5

Negative traits:
Routine	35.1
Boring	2.3
Tiresome	34.1
Frustrating	59.1

The picture will get more complicated when we look at the details, but these parish ministers overwhelmingly find their work valuable, supported, personally enriching. Considering how difficult work situations can be and how much of a gap can exist for people between their values--what they really care about--and the matters and manners that preoccupy them in their work places, it is a real privilege to devote one's life and time to the life and mission of the church community--especially in a setting in which one typically has considerable freedom regarding what one will do and when one will do it. Over 90 percent said that they have sufficient authority to carry out their responsibilities.

Before assembling the full picture, including signals of satisfaction and dissatisfaction from earlier sections, we need to display all the relevant responses from the surveys.

Almost never boring, the work can have its trials and its inherent frustrations, which is the other side of "challenging" and indicates the need for creativity (see table on page 98). But that it is so widely experienced as good and satisfying and respected and almost twice as likely to be fascinating as routine is quite a picture.

FEELINGS ABOUT MINISTRY: PARISH MINISTERS
(percent)

PROPOSITION	Strongly Agree	Agree	Strongly Disagree	Disagree
1. Ministry has been affirming to me.	60.4	33.7	1.4	4.5
2. Ministry has allowed me to develop and to use my talents in the service of the church.	69.6	26.1	1.6	2.7
3. The persons whom I serve have affirmed my worth.	52.1	39.2	1.8	11.1
4. My supervisors in the parish are satisfied with my performance as a lay minister.	46.2	44.1	1.2	8.5
5. Other staff members are satisfied with my performance as a lay minister.	38.8	51.9	0.6	8.7
6. Parishioners are satisfied with my performance as a lay minister.	41.3	50.1	0.2	8.4
7. "Networking" with other ministers has been a personal support to me.	40.2	37.9	3.5	18.4
8. I would encourage others to enter parish ministry.	43.3	39.0	3.7	14

Some other indicators are spelled out in the above table. Ninety percent or more agree with the first six statements and a very small number disagree. (The missing percents are "No opinion or not sure" and no answers.) Even regarding the last two items, very few disagree with the statements; more simply demur. These items are strongly related to each other, the more one agrees with any one item the more s/he agrees with the others. We do need to be concerned that almost one-fifth of the parish ministers are unwilling to say that they would encourage others to join them in parish ministry and we will look at these persons further on.

Put positively, the factors that are most strongly associated with readiness to encourage others to enter parish ministry are items #2, 6, and 5: the feeling of being able to use and develop one's talents, the support from parishioners, and the support from other staff members.

Are there any differences among the various parish ministers? Some. First, there are some differences between the religious and laity on most of these items;

FEELINGS ABOUT PARISH MINISTRY: LAY VS. RELIGIOUS
(percent)

POSITION	Lay		Religious	
	Strongly Agree	Agree	Strongly Agree	Agree
1. Ministry has been affirming to me.	51.1	41.8	72.8	23.0
2. Ministry has allowed me to develop and to use my talents in the service of the church.	66.8	28.6	73.0	23.0
3. The persons whom I serve have affirmed my worth.	45.3	42.4	61.1	35.6
4. My supervisors in the parish are satisfied with my performance as a lay minister.	46.0	43.4	46.5	45.0
5. Other staff members are satisfied with my performance as a lay minister.	36.4	52.7	42.1	51.0
6. Parishioners are satisfied with my performance as a lay minister.	35.7	53.3	49.3	45.8
7. "Networking" with other ministers has been a personal support to me.	40.4	37.3	39.6	39.1
8. I would encourage others to enter parish ministry.	36.2	40.8	52.7	37.1

consistently, the experiences of the religious are more positive than those of the laity, though in some respects by only a few percentage points.[38] On other items a marked difference, sometimes in totals expressing positive sentiments but more often in relative strength of their feelings, exists. The religious are usually and at times much more likely to "strongly agree" with positive statements about parish ministry.

(This is especially true for the full-time parish ministers; the part-timers tend to be more affirmative in general.) The lay persons, for example, are nine points lower than the religious in experiencing that those they serve affirm them. They are fourteen points less likely to encourage others to enter the ministry! When it comes to "strongly agreeing" that they would encourage others, they are sixteen points lower than the religious.

Since parishes will have to rely more and more on the laity for parish ministry, these differences need attention. What other differences are there among the ministers?

SUPPORT IN MINISTRY
(percent working full-time who "Agree" or "Strongly Agree")

POSITION	General Pastoral Minister	Religious Educator	Liturgist	Music Minister	Youth Minister	Other Pastoral Minister
1. Ministry has been affirming to me.	96.2	95.1	90.3	92.3	91.1	94.7
2. Ministry has allowed me to develop and to use my talents in the service of the church.	96.2	96.2	90.3	92.3	95.5	97.4
3. The persons whom I serve have affirmed my worth.	98.1	92.4	83.9	92.3	73.3	94.7
4. My supervisors in the parish are satisfied with my performance as a lay minister.	93.3	91.7	80.6	88.5	86.7	92.1
5. Other staff members are satisfied with my performance as a lay minister.	93.3	91.3	90.3	100.0	80.0	92.1
6. Parishioners are satisfied with my performance as a lay minister.	96.2	91.7	87.1	84.6	88.9	89.5
7. "Networking" with other ministers has been a personal support to me.	82.7	84.8	64.5	77.3	82.2	84.2
8. I would encourage others to enter parish ministry.	90.4	82.6	64.6	61.5	80.0	89.5

In general, differences in level of satisfaction, whether measured as an index combining all the factors we have discussed or simply by the overall appraisal the ministers offer, are little connected to most matters one might expect. The exception is, of course, how well the salary meets the needs of one's family (for lay people) or congregation (for religious). But job descriptions, contracts, staff meetings, and the like seem to have little influence by themselves on satisfaction. [39]

Looked at in terms of the various ministry positions, there are notable differences. Youth ministers seem to derive the least satisfaction and support. The full-time youth ministers find ministry the least affirming, their co-workers the least affirming, their supervisors the least satisfied, parishioners the least satisfied, and youth ministers are least likely to encourage others to enter this ministry. While the number of youth ministers in our sample is rather small--just seventy-three--the consistency of their responses makes us think that this ministry needs particular attention.

The next two least-satisfied groups of ministers appear to be the music ministers and liturgists. The full-time, largely lay music ministers, are not well-satisfied when it comes to co-worker support and use of talents; nor are they ready to encourage others to enter parish ministry. The liturgists, especially the lay persons among them, are even less likely to encourage others to enter parish ministry. Their discontent seems to be focussed on being on their own, not so much on the parish staff, but without a wider network of support. Again, note that this is a small group in the sample--only thirty-eight.

Who are the unhappiest and what makes them unhappy or unsatisfied? We have determined that those who would not "encourage others to enter parish ministry" are the least content. Measured this way, the least content by position are the liturgists (34 percent would not encourage others) and music ministers (32 percent). General pastoral ministers (10 percent)--the majority of whom are religious-- and "others" are the least unhappy. When we compare religious and lay, we find that more lay ministers than religious are among the least content and, among them the liturgy and music ministers stand out. The religious educators and "others" seem most content. When it comes to the men (who are less likely than women to encourage others), contrary to what we found in the other measures of dissatisfaction the youth ministers are more encouraging; recall that half the youth ministers are men. A few other connections are worth reporting: about a third of the divorced and the separated, of the few inactive priests and former religious, and those who thought the position "fit their needs" would not encourage others to enter parish ministry. In short, dissatisfaction, in this measure, is most likely connected either to the positions (liturgy and music) which we have found experience the greatest tension with others and with conditions of the ministers' personal lives (divorce, separation, resignation from priesthood and religious life, and those for whom the fit between their needs and the position was of especial importance).

*   *   *

Care in ensuring clear responsibilities for the parish ministers, in providing just and adequate compensation and working conditions, and in ensuring good communication and support are all important for the future of ministry. These cannot make up for any absence of harmonious personal relationships among all those in parish ministry and especially between the parish ministers and pastors. While the church faces a continuing challenge to foster the personal dispositions as well as the policies and practices that will promote satisfying and effective ministry, what has been accomplished is quite remarkable and a sound basis for further development.

X: Role of the Diocese

Organized efforts to develop and support lay ministry varies considerably from diocese to diocese and ministry to ministry. There is probably no diocese complete in ministry support and there are some that have undertaken extensive efforts for all the elements of lay ministry. We have no exhaustive record or analysis of diocesan activities. We have reports by the lay ministers and their pastors regarding the kinds of help dioceses can and do provide, reports from interviews in the twenty-six dioceses where we conducted site visits, and reports from representatives of about a dozen other dioceses whom we interviewed because of some special development in that diocese.

The services a diocese might provide are the following:

- recruitment and hiring help
- guidelines for ministry positions and respective requirements
- ministry classifications and salary ranges
- assistance with performance reviews and evaluations
- help with job descriptions and contracts
- assistance regarding termination of employment
- education and training for the contents and skills of ministry
- training and consulting help for both the priests and the lay/religious ministers regarding staff development
- ongoing support for the various ministries (resources, networking)
- integration of the lay/religious ministers into the life of the diocese;
- standards of performance for various ministries.

Some poorer parishes also need financial assistance for employing pastoral ministers. Often mentioned was the need for the diocese to provide grievance and conciliation procedures; according to our respondents, about half do.

Most, if not all, dioceses have a history of developing religious education ministry in their parishes. They have established criteria and guidelines for Directors and Coordinators of Religious Education, offered courses for catechists, and established certification procedures. Diocesan guidelines for religious education have evolved over the years and laid the groundwork for much of what has followed for other roles.[40] Some have done the same for youth ministry, establishing their own criteria, training, and certification procedures or drawing on those provided by the Northeast Center for Youth Ministry or some other resource. Even where these supports and guidelines exist, the diocesan directors report that there are always a number of parishes who go their own way, ignoring these policies.

An increasing number of dioceses have organized lay ministry training programs on their own or in cooperation with local educational institutions. Furthermore, many colleges and seminaries have established such programs on their own initiative as a service to the local church. Some of these are degree granting programs, some certification programs.[41] Some are intended to prepare for paid ministry and some for volunteers, but even the latter find that many of their graduates take paid positions in parishes because of their growing interest in doing so and because the pastors in their parishes ask them to do so.[42]

Beyond the education, training, and certification processes, some dioceses have reorganized their personnel offices to take an active role regarding the recruitment, screening, and placement of all pastoral ministers and not just the priests, while others have established lay ministry offices or other structures for responsibility for these new parish ministers.

Reports of Diocesan Support

We asked those in our survey both general and specific questions about diocesan support for lay and religious parish ministry, realizing how broad a category this is, including the well-accepted religious education ministry and music ministry. We asked the pastors their perception of diocesan support for lay ministry. The great majority think that diocesan leadership--the bishop and his associates--are generally in favor of this development: 56.4 percent think the leadership strongly encourages lay parish ministers and 24.7 think they "mildly support" it. Only 1.7 percent think that the leadership is opposed to it and the rest, 17.2 percent, think that the leadership position is not clear. When it comes to direct help to them, 61.8 percent of the pastors and lay persons in parish ministry reported that "in general" the diocese had been helpful to them; the religious in the sample were ten points more likely to report such help, though we must report that many of the pastors and parish ministers in our site visits found the diocesan offices less helpful.

How the diocese was helpful to the three-fifths of those in the survey is less than clear, for when we asked about the role of the diocese in their present placement, only a fifth of all the lay and religious ministers (a quarter of the religious and 16 percent of the lay persons) said that the diocese had played a formal role. Among those dioceses that played a formal role, what was this?

For the twenty percent of religious and lay people in parish ministry regarding whose placement the diocese had played a role, the service provided for a majority of both was the setting of employment policies and salaries. Beyond that, the diocesan role for religious was different from that for lay people. About half of the lay people who found the diocese significant regarding their work in ministry cited the following diocesan services: training programs, certification, screening and recruiting, in that order of frequency. Where the diocesan offices had affected the religious, the services cited by about half were: screening, recruiting, inclusion in diocesan events, and continuing education, in that order. Furthermore, in this limited group, the religious were twice as likely as the laity to point to diocesan commissioning and evaluation of their performance.

Most parishes report that they are largely on their own regarding personnel issues as well as many other issues affecting the new parish ministers.[43] This autonomy means that parishes are unaccountable to the dioceses. It is rather remarkable to find individual parishes drawing up their own personnel policies, procedures, and even contracts without guidance from dioceses, though, as we noted, some ignore the guidance that is there. The situation is changing, however, and we might even say that it is changing rapidly. Increasingly, diocesan offices are serving as clearing-houses for parish ministry positions. More and more are offering training and looking into criteria for certification or at least for parish ministry even without certification.[44] Others have provided financial support for lay persons pursuing ministry education and training.

In some instances, diocesan offices certify religious educators and some other ministries, but in this respect and regarding "commissioning," or some formal deputation for parish ministry by the bishop or his delegate, there appears to be some reluctance to act.[45] Of course, for the bishop or the diocesan office to take this step and, even further, actually appoint someone to a particular ministry position, as occurs regarding priests and deacons, would entail diocesan assumption of considerable responsibility for that minister. On the other hand, not to do so is to leave the situation to a relatively "free market" approach--free-lance ministers accepting positions from autonomous pastors.

Some dioceses have become much more active in providing information to pastors and parishes on good employment practices. The Archdiocese of Seattle has an extensive network of lay ministry formation, employment, and support policies and structures. The Archdiocese of St. Paul-Minneapolis, the Diocese of San Bernadino,[46] and the Archdiocese of Chicago, among others, have published guides for parish personnel practices, each containing both procedures for hiring, employment, and firing and sample job descriptions. The Diocese of Cleveland is in the process of completing its guide, *Parish as Employer*. (It also has an Office of Conciliation that will mediate staff disputes, should they require action beyond the parish.) These dioceses tend also to have a full range of services for parish personnel. Our observer's report on the Archdiocese of St. Paul-Minneapolis was illuminating:

The Office of Ministry serves as a clearinghouse where job openings for all ministries are made available and where prospective employees may file their resumes. Hiring is done on an individual basis by the parish. Some parishes do their own recruiting through national journals such as NCR.

Ministerial training programs leading to degrees are offered by the University of St. Thomas and the College of St. Catherine. Both schools offer Master's Degrees as well as certificate programs.

Diocesan offices provide continued and ongoing in-service to various ministerial groups. Each ministry has it own professional organization that originated in the grass roots but is linked with the diocese. These ministerial associations offer training and in-service programs. In addition there is a coalition of ministries in the diocese which brings together all the individual associations (lay, ordained, religious, parish, institutional, etc.) to explore areas of mutual concern as well as to organize an annual ministry day.

The diocese offers a health plan, pension plan, and has available life insurance and dental plans. While the pension plan is a defined benefit plan a portion of the contribution made by the parish for each employee is returned to the employee in the form of a TDA. The Archdiocese has published personnel guidelines for parishes, a manual for personnel practices and job descriptions. In addition, the Archdiocese has a grievance procedure for handling disputes. All employees are hired directly by the parish. Interviewing, contracts, salaries are all handled at the local level, not by the diocese, though the diocese does provide information regarding prevailing wages for the various ministries. This archdiocese is strongly committed to lay ministry. In 1984 it established an Office of Ministry under the direction of a lay woman who is one of the five members of the archbishop's council.[47]

The Archdiocese of St. Paul-Minneapolis has also given special and perhaps unique attention to a particular lay ministry that proves to be of great help to pastors, that of the Parish Business Administrator.[48] These are the ministers we have discussed above, who take on much of the responsibility for the management concerns of the parish: schedules, purchasing and cash disbursements, communications, oversight of maintenance, and other matters. More than any other minister, these persons relieve the pastor of the management concerns that usurp time and attention from more directly pastoral concerns. It turns out that many of the participants in this program come from the military or from a small business background. They often need good formation in ecclesiology to help them shift from the business "culture" to the church culture and values.

Others have recognized the need to do long-range planning to face a future with many fewer priests. The Diocese of San Angelo, for example, after spelling out future trends in ministry, has established "Norms Governing Pastoral Coordinators/ Associates"--qualification, education, job descriptions, contract elements, and supervision for non-ordained parish leaders, which are included in the Diocesan Pastoral Manual--and a twenty year plan for staffing parishes--detailed schemes for inter-parish cooperation, gradually engaging clusters of parishes. Prior to this a lay ministry training program was established, which has attracted a large number of people and the religious education department developed a three-year program, working with both paid and volunteer coordinators.

Hierarchical and Peer Support

A number of the lay ministers we interviewed looked to the bishop for support. It seems important to include these ministers in appropriate diocesan events, those that concern diocesan pastoral matters in which they are directly involved. Quite disappointing to them have been occasions where all the priests in a particular ministry or a particular region (deanery) were invited to a meeting on pastoral matters but the lay/religious ministers were not invited. *Examples include one meeting of campus ministers to which the three priests were invited but the sister was not.*

Aside from the bishop's support, the pastoral ministers are generally grateful when there is a support group of their peers--meetings of DRE's or pastoral associates or youth ministers or the like. A little over half the parish ministers say they participate in a form of diocesan support group, about a third in a regional organization of some kind, and a little over a quarter in a national organization(s). Whether through such organized groups or with other individuals of their own choosing, more than three-quarters of the parish ministers agree with the statement: "'Networking' with other ministers has been a personal support to me." When there is no such support group, they can often feel quite isolated.

The older ministries--religious education and youth ministry--seem to have the best organized "support groups." Lacking these, the general pastoral ministers seem equally to have found support on their own, but the liturgists are less likely to have such groups. The liturgists often share an advantage with religious education and youth ministry, however: a diocesan office to which they can confidently relate, an office looking out for their interests and well disposed to understand their concerns.

Where support groups are lacking, the ministers themselves seem to be developing them, *groups such as the Pastoral Minister Support Group in one diocese and the Professional Pastoral Ministers Association which has 140 members in another diocese. The latter group is very active both in continuing ministry development of their own members and in promoting good personnel policies and procedures in the diocese and its parishes. Because of the association's activity to improve working conditions, some priests have referred to it as a "union" and the coordinator as a "shop steward."*

Another service a diocese might provide is in the area of conciliation, grievance resolution, due process. Fifty-one percent of the lay and religious ministers report that their diocese or parish already has "a grievance procedure;" 38 percent said they did not, and the remaining 11 percent did not reply to the question.[49] Some arrangements will be increasingly important, arrangements that provide not only for handling situations where the parties seem unable to achieve reconciliation themselves, but also for reducing the need for such procedures. We have already noted that many ministers find themselves poorly equipped for managing conflict; undoubtedly the priests feel the same. Some regular minister and staff training in this respect, linked with the encouragement of good policies and practices among parish staffs, could enable them to work through more of these difficulties. Nonetheless, when this is not possible, both the claims of justice and the need to encourage lay ministers to remain committed to church ministry will call for good procedures for handling grievances.[50]

It seems rather inevitable that dioceses will become more active regarding lay and parish ministers in order to protect the ministry and the ministers. Based on past experience, where the pastors and parishes have been so creative and responsible, any diocesan initiative might do well to involve the pastors in the planning and to maintain some balance between diocesan and parish responsibility. One might also anticipate that steps taken to ensure justice and good stewardship regarding lay and religious personnel will have a tendency to affect the clergy as well--the policies and practices affecting them and the involvement of the parishioners regarding clergy appointments. This is already evident in the parishes themselves where parish pastoral and finance councils are discussing such matters as ministry accountability and evaluation, as well as provision of working spaces and supports for pastors and lay and religious parish ministers alike.

XI: Accomplishments and Challenges

The intent of this study was to determine "what helps and hinders" the participation by lay people and religious in parish ministry. The previous chapters have offered answers to that question as well as to other questions, especially, how have lay and religious parish ministers contributed to parish ministry? It is not our role or intent to make specific policy recommendations at this point; we leave them to the subcommittee of the bishops' Committee on Pastoral Research and Practices. Nonetheless, it is appropriate for us to pull together the threads of our research in this final chapter as preparation for those recommendations.

Accomplishments

From the beginning the subcommittee and consultants for the bishops spoke as if the introduction of lay people and religious into parish ministry was not only a necessary development but a desirable one. At no time were we asked to find out whether this was a good practice. Our research confirmed what we inferred from their comments: from all measures, lay and religious parish ministers have been a great boon to parish ministry. They feel they have contributed to many parts of parish community and mission, and the pastors and parishioners with whom they serve agree. Of great importance is that they have enabled the parish to reach more people, but they have also contributed to religious education, liturgy, spirituality, hospitality and pastoral care. They have brought their education, their skill, their sensitivities, and their experience to parish ministry.

It is further tribute to them and the pastors who have hired them that this development has gone so smoothly and that the parish ministers find the opportunity to minister so satisfying. For the vast majority of them do. They report broad support from all sides: the pastors, other ministers, and parishioners. The best evidence of their satisfaction is that the majority of them would encourage others to enter parish ministry.

The mixed background and characteristics of these parish ministers is also a tribute to pastoral ingenuity and openness of the parishes. For they include not only religious and lay, but also people of considerable difference of education and background, full-time ministers with considerable professional preparation and parishioners with little specific ministry formation. This can create problems: not ensuring enough preparation for some, or not assuring adequate respect and working conditions for those who have worked hard at professional preparation. Yet, it is also an accomplishment of inclusion and integration.

What fosters this development? What seem to be the obstacles or at least the inhospitable conditions for it?

Ministry Environment

Certain environmental factors are important--parish locale and composition, income and size, to name a few of these factors. First, some dioceses and areas of the country seem more "open" or "committed," or whatever the apt expression is, to lay/religious parish ministry. These dioceses, through their ministry formation programs, their continuing education, their personnel practices, and the focus of their diocesan offices, welcome these ministers to their parishes. This openness may extend to active promotion reflected in structures and practices such as: diocesan personnel offices which formally have responsibility for all pastoral ministers and not just for the priests; diocesan commissioning and even appointment of lay and religious ministers to particular parishes; inclusion of parish ministers in appropriate meetings, committees, and events. Other dioceses are not so "proactive" but are quite hospitable to these ministers. To be sure, there is hardly a diocese that does not welcome lay and religious ministers for religious education positions, as parish visitors, or as music ministers. It is in their disposition toward the more general roles of pastoral associate or parish minister or the particular roles of liturgy director, catechumenate director, or others that differences of disposition are most evident. Some dioceses, and parishes, are more accepting than welcoming of these women and men into the recent pastoral ministries, conveying the impression that these ministers are a necessary and temporary substitute for priests; others convey that these ministers are valuable in themselves. The basic stance of a diocese and its assurance of policies and practices that protect ministry and ministers are obviously related. We will consider more about the dioceses below.

Second, the larger parishes and those with greater financial resources are better able to hire parish ministers, whether or not they have parish schools. The smaller parishes and poorer parishes that have schools often cannot hire parish ministers. The smaller parishes may often not need such ministers, but their needs and constraints should be considered in any ministry planning.

Third, the competition between schools and religious education programs should be put to rest. The budget for religious education, or at least a parish's readiness to hire religious educators, is not usually affected by the presence of a school. Parish financial commitment to religious education is a separate matter and needs separate attention.

Fourth, to some degree parish staffing needs are measured by programs more than persons. By this we mean that the larger parishes do not hire ministers in proportion to the number of Catholics or even of active Catholics. The ministers seem hired more to manage the programs than to reach all the Catholics, though the two are related. A good and potentially fruitful discussion might be held regarding the relationship between hiring staff and promoting parishioner responsibility (what has come to be understood as the ministerial responsibility of all the baptized and to be called an aspect of stewardship) for the cares and works of a parish community.

Pastors

Almost all our work confirms the importance of the pastor. This is not surprising. The pastor is leader of the parish and his approach to the ministry and staffing will be determinative, especially regarding a development that has been left largely to the parish level. The appendix to Chapter 5 was a glimpse of variations in style among pastors who have good relationships with their lay and religious ministers. There is no one quality among pastors, as there is no one style of parish minister, that best serves the development of lay parish ministry. We have come to conclude that the best arrangements comprise style and structure: the manners in which people relate to one another and the ways they organize these relationships.

Whatever the combination of style and structure, and not overlooking the problems that exist, the pastors have done a remarkable job. This is the report of the parish ministers. The majority have found their pastors supportive, accessible, and cooperative. A remarkable percentage can count on the structural supports of: job description, contracts, and staff meetings for clear responsibilities and good communication. They further characterize their relationship with their pastors in the positive terms of "friend," "colleague," and "staff member." A few feel reduced to the level of "employee." If there is a common failing parish ministers find in pastors, it may be where the personal and organizational come closer together. Thus some ministers would like more organized occasions when they could pray together, look for more socializing among the staff, miss personal evaluations, and look for more personal praise and encouragement of their efforts than pastors are wont to express. Parish ministers admit their own poor preparation for handling conflict and achieving collaboration and, though we did not ask them, the ongoing contact we have with priests assures us that priests would admit to similar gaps in their formation.

The new roles of pastors as "personnel managers" in the very small circle of a parish staff, combined with the new expectations of healthy and cooperative work relationships with women and lay men, warrant assistance through continuing education and staff development services. Where such opportunities for personal reflection, training in appropriate skills, and guides for good staff structures have been made available, pastors have responded enthusiastically. What the appropriate relationships--personal, organizational, spiritual, and social--will be vary with the individuals involved and will continue to evolve; we have seen evidence of increasing realism in ministers' and pastors' expectations of each other. Guidelines and training can help all involved to make what we have recognized as the autonomy of each parish not an excuse for arbitrary and unfair arrangements, to say nothing of unjust and illegal ones.

Monitoring the use of job descriptions and contracts should help the church to discover what is helpful and appropriate to the parish work situation. It is not to be taken for granted that either in their present forms serves all the parishes and parish ministers' needs.

Background and Preparation for Ministry

The great majority of the new ministers are women and about half of them are women religious. The women religious have broken new ground and continue to do so, since they occupy most of the "new" roles, those of pastoral associate and pastoral minister--what we have called general parish ministers--just as they had led the way in religious education. Their numbers will diminish with their advancing age and the lack of many replacements coming after them. They have brought considerable education, spirituality, and experience--especially in teaching--to this ministry. They will continue to make a contribution to parish life and in the future will be sorely missed. The graduate schools for ministerial preparation report a declining number of women religious students and a shift to a majority of lay students. They also attest to the difficulty of having enough lay students able to pay their way and then find their way in ministry.

The lay counterparts are also well educated and make a great contribution, whether they are part-time or full-time employees, though they are not so well educated, particularly in theology and related religious studies as the sisters have been. While the majority of them and their pastors feel their preparation and performance regarding theological and religious studies are adequate, a good percentage of them feel the need for further education in doctrine, moral theology, Scripture, and liturgy. The shift from religious to lay also means that, where the religious congregations took responsibility for their members' education and formation, this burden for assuring adequate preparation appears to shift to the parish and diocese. The religious congregations also provide back-up for their members who lose their positions for one reason or another; the lay ministers lacking any "order"--by vows or ordination--are essentially left to their own devices. Undoubtedly, all the advantages the religious enjoy play some part in their generally experiencing greater satisfaction and effectiveness in their work.

Continuing preparation for all ministers, full-time and part-time, in the substantive areas of ministry as well as in the skills necessary for the works and relationships of ministry can be a great help. For parishioners, and especially part-timers among them, these offerings can have the added value of seeing their ministry in the context of the larger church and broader development of their particular ministries. Among the skills needed will be the ability to motivate and invite parishioners into ministry, to organize and supervise the work of others, and to be able to counsel parishioners.

We should relate this emergence of ministry to another much discussed phenomenon in the church, namely, the emergence of generations of Catholics with less socialization in the Catholic tradition and community. Smaller percentages of Catholics participate regularly in the sacramental life of the church or attend Catholics schools. This has already been faced by seminary faculties and will be an issue among lay ministers as well.

Finally, parish and diocesan leaders will need to redouble their efforts to recruit, train, and support many more African-American and Hispanic ministers if we are to serve the parishes of the future.

All in all, the education and formation for lay ministry may be too important to be left as unorganized as at present.

Working Conditions

The parish ministers report that their working conditions are quite satisfactory; pastors are more critical of the conditions they provide for these ministers. The two conditions that warrant most attention are space and money.

Ministry works best when there is adequate working space for the parish ministers and when the priests can reasonably segregate this shared working space from their own living space. Newer parish buildings are being accommodated to these needs; reorganization of older facilities can be quite inventive and helpful.

Salaries and health benefits will always be a struggle for parishes as they are for most non-profit organizations. At the same time, if other research is to be trusted, on the one hand, the income of the average Catholic exceeds that of most others in our society and, on the other hand, Catholics give a steadily smaller percentage of their incomes than their forebears and than those of other churches. Efforts to increase Catholic parish support may be not only necessary but possible to support adequate compensation for parish ministers.

Particular Ministries

Some parishes will continue to hire specialists, especially musicians. For most parishes, however, the future seems to lie in a combination of general parish ministers--pastoral associates, pastoral ministers, parish ministers, whatever the terms used, and religious educators. As some former religious educators suspected, most of these general roles do entail responsibility for religious education in addition to many other ministries. There will undoubtedly be continuing need to integrate these general parish ministers into the pastoral planning and coordinating efforts of dioceses.

The more specialized ministers who have the greatest difficulty working out their positions in parishes are the liturgists and musicians. These difficulties can be interpreted by those involved as "personality" clashes, but when they are part of a pattern they warrant more consideration than that. Exploratory reflections among pastors, pastoral liturgists and musicians, and others might locate ways to prepare those involved for more harmonious and fruitful relationships.

Another role that has emerged and has been found very helpful is that of the parish manager, the person who sees to many of the organizational and resource needs of parishes. Parish managers can relieve the pastor of this work and enhance orderly communication between staff and parishioners as well as among the staff themselves.   Given the increasingly technical and legal elements of parish administration, investment in this ministry could result in greater support for pastors and parish ministers and good protection against financial and legal problems. Though poor parishes are often least able to afford this help, their often burdensome plants and broad expectations of pastors would especially warrant it.

*   *   *

What has evolved so freely as a result of the openness and interest in good church ministry on the part of laity, religious, and clergy alike may now require greater assistance and support from dioceses, religious orders, and national offices and organizations. What appears desirable is the kind of help that ensures respect for all involved, that provides assurance of good ministry and good treatment as a minister, and that both encourages the kind of creativity among pastors and parish ministers that has been so fruitful in the past decades while ensuring the good order of the church.

Notes

1. Cf. "The New Parish," pp. 16-17, unpublished ms. by Philip J. Murnion, 1982, initial report on the first phase of the Notre Dame Study of Catholic Parish Life.

2. Ibid., p. 17.

3. Of course the transition from religious (and clergy) to lay personnel has taken place much earlier in parish schools. One study found that the parents saw no appreciable difference between the performance of lay teachers and religious; cf. Anthony S. Bryk, Peter Holland, Valerie E. Lee, and Ruben A. Carriedo, *Effective Catholic Schools: An Exploration*, 1984, National Center for Research in Total Catholic Education.

4. The Notre Dame Study found that, when parishioners were asked to identify the primary leaders of parish ministries, 83 percent of these leaders were lay people; cf. David C. Leege and Joseph Gremillion, *The U.S. Parish Twenty Years After Vatican II: An Introduction to the Study*, Report No. 1, December 1984.

5. A helpful analysis of some differences between men and women, differences which we find reflected in approaches to parish ministry, is Walter Ong, *Fighting for Life*, Amherst, Univ. of Massachusett Press, 1989. An analysis of the eulogies preached at priests' funerals in the early part of the century finds the virtue of "courage" often mentioned, reflecting this view that the parish priest's ministry involved some danger and challenge; see Philip J. Murnion, *The Catholic Priest and the Changing Structure of Pastoral Ministry*, New York, Arno Press, 1978; p. 87.

6. One effort to explore some of these relationships has been undertaken as a hearing process by Glenmary brothers and priests with the women who work in their parishes, cf., Evelyn Dettling, *Co-Ministry as a Process*, 1986, National Federation of Priests' Councils. The writer finds that the qualities most effective for co-ministering were sharing and trust, suffering[?], openness to transformation, while those that seemed to affect the quality of ministering were the styles of leadership and structures for action.

7. We might note here that committees of the National Conference of Catholic Bishops have long labored to develop an acceptable taxonomy for ministry, at one point restricting the term to those ordained or in some way formally deputed for a significant, long-term pastoral role in the church as distinct from the Christian witness of all the baptized, but this distinction became a problem when Pope John Paul II ascribed the responsibility of "ministry" to all members of a family in *Familiaris consortio*. The matter remains unresolved.

8. Andrew Abbott, *The System of Professions*, Chicago, Univ. of Chicago Press, 1988.

9. Compensation of persons in ministry has been the object of some recent studies. *Just Wages and Benefits for Lay and Religious Church Employees* is the report of a joint project of numerous church organizations coordinated by the National Conference of Diocesan

Directors of Religious Education with the assistance of Lilly Endowment. We will draw on the final report published in 1991 later in this report. Earlier FADICA (Foundations and Donors Interested in Catholic Activities) had conducted a symposium on the subject of lay ministry; the final report points to the challenge of providing adequate salaries.   See FADICA, *Laity in Catholic Ministry: Moving into the Future*, Washington, D.C., FADICA, 1987. An analysis of the relative costs of laity, religious, and clergy in parish ministry is found in Dean Hoge, Jackson Carroll, and Francis Scheets, *Patterns of Parish Leadership*, Kansas City, Sheed and Ward, 1988.

10. Roberto O. Gonzalez and Michael Lavelle, *The Hispanic Catholic in the United States: A Socio-Cultural and Religious Profile*, New York, Northeast Catholic Pastoral Center for Hispanics, 1985, concludes that involvement in parish leadership is strongly related to prior parish involvement and that the overwhelming majority of Hispanic Catholics are not actively involved in their parishes. See also Juan Hurtado, *An Attitudinal Study of Social Distance between The Mexican American and the Church*, unpublished doctoral dissertation, United States International University, 1975, where it is also argued that "distance" (as a sociological measure) of the Mexican American from the institutional structures of the church make the prospect of more Mexican American church leadership not very likely.

11. Cf. Eugene Hemrick, *A National Study of the Permanent Diaconate in the United States*, Washington, D.C., United States Catholic Conference, 1981.

12. Some dioceses like Miami have made a concentrated effort to develop Hispanic lay ministers. The Archdiocese of Chicago has cooperated with Catholic Theological Union to promote African-American ministry by making scholarship money available.

13. The relationship between staff development and the pastor's leadership style has also been argued in one of the fascicles reporting the Notre Dame Study of Catholic Parish Life: David C. Leege, *Parish Organizations: People's Needs, Parish Services, and Leadership*, Report No. 8, July, 1986.

14. See David C. Leege and Thomas A. Trozzolo, "Participation in Catholic Parish Life: Religious Rites and Parish Activities in the 1980's," *Notre Dame Study*, Report No. 3, 1985, pp. 6-7.

15. Another study suggests that parish ministers, by their own choice, do not stay long in a given parish; see Zenobia V. Fox, *A Post-Vatican II Phenomenon: Lay Ministries: A Critical Three-Dimensional Study*, unpublished dissertation, Fordham University, 1986, p. 65. Further sections of this dissertation are valuable for comparison with the present study as well as for matters not treated in the present study.

16. Much valuable information about the specifically lay (as distinguished from religious) parish ministers can be found in Zenobia Fox, "The New Parish Ministers," *CHURCH*, 7:1 (Spring 1991), pp. 16-21.

17. One author suggests that lay people will not have access to the more "professional" positions; these will be filled by religious. The lack of openness to lay professionals is attributed to what the author sees as unwillingness of parish priests to share responsibility. See Patricia Wittberg, "The Dual Labor Market in the Catholic Church; Expanding a Speculative Inquiry," *Review of Religious Research*, March 1989. As we will discuss further, we regard this as an inadequate description of the priests and explanation of the patterns of hiring.

18. A study of Black Catholics found that leadership training of Black Catholics is a critical need for the church if there are to be more black persons in leadership positions; cf. Bangass and Associates, *National Survey on Black Catholic Life*, Washington, D.C., National Office of Black Catholics, 1986.

19. In this vein, Cardinal William Baum of the Congregation of Seminaries and Universities has cautioned against too early an acceptance into seminaries of people who, because of a strong emotional experience in their lives, "come to a heightened consciousness of God" and "can easily mistake that consciousness for a call to the priesthood." See Cardinal William W. Baum, "The State of U.S. Free-Standing Seminaries," *Origins* 16:18 (October 16, 1986), p. 318.

20. The directors of the Institute for Religious Education and Pastoral Ministry at Boston College and of the Extension Program at Loyola of New Orleans noted that some of their students came from these programs that deepened their faith and church commitment.

21. Some earlier studies of preparation of laity for church ministry are: Suzanne E. Elsesser and Eugene F. Hemrick, *Preparing Laity for Ministry: A Report on Programs in Catholic Dioceses Throughout the United States*, 1986, Bishops' Committee on the Laity and Office of Research, NCCB/USCC, which incudes degree and certification and other programs; and Louise Bond, "An Evaluation of Lay Ministry Training," 1988, unpublished paper.

22. The National Federation for Catholic Youth Ministry has published "NFCYM Competency-Based Standards for the Coordinator of Youth Ministry." These standards were approved by the United States Catholic Conference Commission on Certification and Accreditation. These "standards" include required knowledge and competencies in a variety of areas including spirituality, theology, management, and youth development. We could not help but notice a rather formal approach to some areas, e.g., doctrine, and a curious tendency to accept some prevailing theologies of youth and religious development a little more than church teaching. Thus, the section on moral theology and decision making requires knowledge of "the scriptural foundations for Catholic moral teaching, conscience formation, and theological reflection on Catholic moral teachings," and "understanding of principles of Catholic morality," as well as competencies in teaching young people processes for making moral decisions as Catholic Christians, for **reflecting critically on Catholic moral teachings** [emphasis added], and for utilizing Catholic moral principles in their decision making," and in "ability to design and implement youth learning experiences in the areas of morality, sexuality, and moral decision making." When it comes to the section on adolescent development, the youth minister is to know all about the

stages and theories and to apply them but there is nothing about critical thinking regarding these theories.

23. One study of sisters moving from educational ministry to other ministries is Julia Ann Heslin, *In Transition: A Study of Women Religious Administrators in Non-traditional Roles*, unpublished dissertation, Fordham University, 1983.

24. The director of one of the major graduate programs for pastoral ministry also reported the challenge they at the school face in training students who lack a strong background in the theology and community of the church, a problem shared by seminary faculties educating seminarians with similarly shallow background in the church.

25. One study of directors of religious education has documented their failure to attract adequate professional recognition because of the great diversity in professional credentials among those being hired for the position; see Thomas P. Walters, *DRE Issues and Concerns for the 80's*, National Conference of Diocesan Directors of Religious Education, 1983. See also Thomas Walters, *National Profile of Professional Religious Education Coordinators/Directors*, National Conference of Diocesan Directors of Religious Education, 1983.

26. Regarding the importance of a pastor's support, see Thomas P. Walters, *National Profile of Religious Education Coordinators/Directors*. Walters found that the primary reason that some DREs leave a parish position was lack of support from their pastors; cf. Pat Pintens, "Why DREs Relocate," PACE, 1985. According to Walters, the pastor's support was important not only for a satisfying working situation for the religious educators but for the effectiveness of the religious education program itself. Further evidence of the importance of the pastor's support is reported in Francis D. Kelly, Peter L. Benson, and Michael J. Donahue, *Toward Effective Parish Religious Education for Children and Young People: A National Study*, National Catholic Education Association, 1986.

27. Toni Falbo, B. Lynn New, and Margie Gaines, "Perceptions of Authority and the Power Strategies Used by Clergymen," *Journal for the Scientific Study of Religion*, December, 1987, found that Catholic priests tend to utilize what they call (borrowing from Max Weber) a "legal-rational" approach to authority using planning and goal setting, program development and implementation, and the like as ways to establish order.

28. This matches the NACPA survey, which seems to find parish "employees" having job descriptions at about the same frequency; see Lucien Roy, "Attitudinal Survey on Working in the Catholic Church: Recruitment, Job Descriptions, Performance Appraisals," NACPA newsletter, *Church Personnel Issues*, June 1991, pp. 2ff.

29. The NACPA survey finds that priests are less likely than others to have a job description. This is undoubtedly because most of them are in supervisory positions for which job descriptions are less likely and because in this respect they operate more like professionals for whom job descriptions are less likely. The general parish ministers share some of this broad and professional responsibility as distinct from the more narrowly defined role of an employee which may explain why they are the least likely to have job

descriptions.

The Archdiocese of Boston has produced a set of guidelines for the general pastoral ministers, "Guidelines for Pastoral Associates," Office for Pastoral Ministries, 1989.

30. Virgil C. Funk, *An NPM Workbook: Job Descriptions, Contracts, Salary*, Washington, D.C., NPM Publications, 1988.

31. See "DRE Yesterday, Today, Tomorrow," produced by the Joint Steering Committee on National Standards for Parish Directors of Religious Education [of NCDD and NCEA].

32. The NACPA material seems to link "professionalization" with job descriptions and evaluations--this is not self-evident. The latter may be more a function of bureaucratization than professionalization (cf. Lucien Roy, op. cit., p. 6). See also the concern about lay vocation in Lucien Roy, op cit., p. 7.

33. Two perspectives on staff collaboration have been sketched by Matthias Neuman in "Collaboration: Expectations and Obstacles," *CHURCH*, 3:2 (Summer 1987), pp. 5-10 and "Five Virtues of Collaborative Ministry," *CHURCH*, 4:4 (Winter 1988), pp. 10-16. An approach to collaboration that focuses more on the relationship between staff and parishioners can be found in Loughlan Sofield, S.T. and Carroll Juliano, S.H.C.J., *Collaborative Ministry*, Notre Dame, IN., Ave Maria Press, 1987.

34. One study already cited which pointed to the difficulty of measuring effectiveness in ministry--in this instance, religious education ministry--because of the absence of agreed standards and clear goals is Thomas P. Walters, *DRE Issues and Concerns for the 80's.*

35. National Conference of Catholic Bishops, Committee on the Parish, *The Parish: A People, A Mission, A Structure*, Washington, D.C., USCC Publications, 1981.

36. An earlier study of directors of religious education had suggested that these directors themselves could not agree on the qualities of a good Catholic Christian which might give direction to their work. The researcher further suggested that this lack of consensus may account for what he perceived to be some differences of criteria for good religious education between directors of religious education and parents. See Thomas P. Walters, "Challenge to the DRE: The Search for a Systematic and Total Parish Catechesis," *Living Light*, 1985. Another study discerned some features related to effective programs of religious education such as good staff-volunteer relationships, on-going recruitment and training for catechists, shared planning with parish councils and religious education boards, and pastors' support; see Kelly, Benson, Donahue, op. cit.

37. See Dean R. Hoge, Jackson W. Carroll, and Francis K. Scheets, OSC, *Patterns of Parish Leadership*, Kansas City: Sheed and Ward, 1988, pp. 98 ff. See also, Dean R. Hoge, *The Future of Catholic Leadership*, Kansas City: Sheed and Ward, 1987.

38. A study in one diocese also found among directors of religious education that the women religious reported much higher job satisfaction than did the lay women in these positions; cf. Patricia McNicholas, "The Parish Director of Religious Education and the

School Principal," Diocese of Youngstown, April, 1984.

39. This is contrary to the NACPA finding that there is a strong connection between satisfaction and having a job description (though we need to note that "satisfaction" is measured inferentially in that study, a composite of three items regarding "my involvement in ministry," "the responsibility I have been given," and "the recognition I receive from my work"); see Lucien Roy, op. cit., p. 4.

40. See, for example, Archdiocese of Chicago, *Parish Religious Education Policies and Guidelines*, 1990.

41. See the directory of these programs produced by the Secretariat for the Laity of the National Conference of Catholic Bishops, Elsesser and Hemrick, op. cit.

42. Sr. Joan Bland, founder of Education for Parish Service in Washington, D.C. and other cities reports this experience among the graduates of the two-year program, as do other program directors.

43. A couple of good examples of parishes which have developed comprehensive policies and procedures for parish ministers and ministries are the parish of St. Thomas the Apostle in Old Bridge, New Jersey (Diocese of Metuchen), where the pastor Monsignor John Szymanski has organized a thorough set of policies, practices and job descriptions; and Church of the Sacred Heart in Boise, Idaho whose "Procedural Manual" organized by Father W. Thomas Faucher systematizes parish management and all the positions in the parish including that of the pastor.

44. One study of diocesan and college-based lay ministry programs in Ohio has found that many persons enrolled not directly to prepare for some formal position but because the program offered adult religious education. (This same experience in other parts of the country has been reported by Ms. Dolores Leckey, Secretary of the Office of Laity of the National Conference of Catholic Bishops.) Nonetheless, having entered for that reason, some of the participants then considered the possibility of taking a more active role in parish or other ministry. The openness of these programs to varying interests may welcome more lay persons into pastoral ministry. See James M. Utendorf, *The Motivational Orientations of Participants in Roman Catholic Lay Ministry Training Programs*, unpublished dissertation, Graduate Department of Educational Theory, The Ontario Institute for Studies in Education, 1987.

45. There are, of course, many exceptions to this, even apart from the commissioning of Eucharistic Ministers. Many dioceses have had a form of certification for religious education directors, coordinators, and catechists, for youth ministers and for other ministries (cf., for example, the scheme for "Diocesan Certification for Pastoral Ministry" of the Diocese of Cleveland). Formal commissioning has been less frequent, but some dioceses (Green Bay and Seattle, among others) have a fairly comprehensive approach to this.

46. Diocese of San Bernadino, *Guidelines for Coordinating Parish Ministries: A Handbook for Parish Staffs*, 1988.

47. Site visit report from the Archdiocese of St. Paul-Minneapolis.

48. See also the guidelines for parish business manager in the Diocese of Green Bay, Wisconsin; Diocese of Green Bay, *Commissioned Ministry Formation: Program Handbook*, pp. 5 and 22.

49.   The NACPA survey found that a third of the parish "employees" (again including more than the pastoral ministers) rejected the view that if they had a legitimate grievance about working conditions, the church would treat them justly. See William P. Daly and Ann Marie Winters, "Attitudinal Survey on Working in the Catholic Church: Employment Grievances," NACPA newsletter, *Church Personnel Issues*, August 1991, p. 4. For a review of diocesan due process procedures, see James Provost, ed., *Due Process in Dioceses in the United States 1970-1985: Report on a Survey*, Washington, D.C., Canon Law Society of America, 1987.

50. See Ann Marie Winters, "A Systemic Approach for Just Handling of Grievances," in Daly and Winters, op. cit, pp. 10-12.

Appendix A: Lay Men in Ministry

Lay Men in Ministry

David DeLambo

Because 85 percent of the parish ministers surveyed were women, we became aware that the *New Parish Ministers* study primarily reflected the backgrounds, attitudes and experiences of women in pastoral ministry. Consequently, we felt the need to surface the distinctive but submerged profile of the non-ordained men. This was not possible among the religious where brothers comprised less than two percent of all religious in parish ministry. There were simply not enough of them to make valid generalizations. But such was not the case among the laity where about one in four ministers were men. This appendix will therefore contrast lay men to lay women in parish ministry, noting areas of divergence while providing an overview of lay ministry as a whole.

Background

That lay men in parish ministry are few in number is quite well known, but that they are younger as well comes as a surprise. The average age for lay men is 39, while for women it's 46. And the difference is more pronounced than the figures indicate, for half the men (50 percent) are age 35 or younger compared to 12 percent of the women. Among youth ministers the disparity is most dramatic: 84 percent of the men versus 18 percent of the women are 35 or younger.

Yet despite their youth, men have served in their current ministry positions an average of six years, about the same length of time as the women surveyed. Age apparently has little to do with one's length of time in a particular job, though we don't know if ministers held the same job at a different parish, or worked in their current parish in a different capacity.

Men are significantly less likely to be married (44 percent vs. 70 percent of the women). Given their relative youth, this might be expected, for the majority of ministers 35 or younger are single. But youth does not explain everything. The proportion of married men 35 and under is still quite small (28 percent vs. 44 percent of women), relatively speaking.

Besides being "younger" and "single," men are "highly educated" (see accompanying table). Nearly all lay men (91 percent) have at least a bachelor's degree versus about two-thirds of the women and roughly half have a master's degree or better while fewer than a third of women do. Also, 10 percent of men have earned doctorates compared to three-tenths of one percent of the women. The men are a highly educated group indeed.

Of course level of education, like marital status, varies with age. One finds, for example, that women age 35 and under have education levels closer to those of men. But before one assumes that the young are better educated as a whole, a look at those over 35 will complicate the picture. Men over 35 have a higher level of education than younger men, with a greater proportion having

LAY EDUCATIONAL BACKGROUND:
MEN VS. WOMEN
(percent)

LEVEL OF EDUCATION	Men	Women
High school or less	2.0	8.8
Some college or other post high school	7.0	26.3
College graduate	22.0	18.4
Some graduate work	19.0	16.8
Master's degree	33.0	29.4
M.Div.	7.0	0.0
D.Min.	2.0	0.3
Doctorate	10.0	0.3

bachelor's and master's degrees. But women over 35, while having a slightly higher proportion with their master's, have three times as many *without* a bachelor's degree (38 percent vs. 13 percent).

Differences in work experience prior to ministry are also evident. Few enter ministry directly or have worked as ministers exclusively. The vast majority (about 70 percent) were formerly employed full-time in a field other than church ministry. Of the men that were, more than four in five worked as professionals (85 percent), mostly in the profit-making sector (58 percent). Women's experience is more diverse. Fewer served as professionals (65 percent), and those that did worked mainly in the not-for-profit realm (69 percent) which includes public service agencies. Those women not employed as professionals (35 percent) held support staff positions, again, mainly in not-for-profit organizations.

Ministry Positions

POSITIONS HELD BY LAY MINISTERS:
MEN vs. WOMEN
(percent)

POSITION	Men	Women
General Pastoral Ministers	18.0	13.7
Religious Educators	23.0	61.7
Liturgists	5.0	5.7
Music Ministers	28.0	6.0
Youth Ministers	25.0	9.8
Other Pastoral Ministers	1.0	3.0

Perhaps the greatest difference between the two groups resides in the positions they are likely to hold. As can be seen in the accompanying table, lay women overwhelmingly serve as religious educators: nearly two-thirds of them do, whereas lay men are spread more evenly over a number of positions. Music ministry, youth ministry and religious education each account for about a quarter of the men, while general pastoral ministry makes up about a fifth.

Why such dissimilarity among the types of positions held? The type of work the ministers engaged in prior to their current pastoral roles plays a part. Among religious educators, for example, 52 percent have had previous experience in Catholic education either as teachers or administrators or in some other form of ministry at the parish school. For them the move from parish school to parish ministry is not so much a change in occupation as a change in orientation and location, especially if they taught religion. The non-school position provides an alternative, creative, less structured environment -- apparently one with some appeal.

That the vast majority of religious educators are women follows from the gender profile of teachers. Education is a field women have come to dominate. Until recently --along with nursing and secretarial work-- they had few occupational alternatives. In church circles the same was true. Religious education was the first and, for years, only pastoral position open to women. It will be interesting to see what effect the growing demand for general pastoral ministers will have on the concentration of women in religious education.

While women are far more likely to serve as religious educators than men, men are far more likely to serve as music ministers (28 percent) than women (6 percent). And one must suspect that the domination of men in the music professions --composing, performing, conducting-- like the domination of women in the education field, plays into this.

Youth ministry is a different story. Although the second highest percentage of men work as youth ministers, women slightly outnumber men in this ministry. But the relatively equal numbers of men and women make youth ministry among the most balanced of the pastoral positions. Unlike religious education and music ministry, who is in youth ministry has less to do with previous employment and professional training, and more to do with having had formative experiences in youth movements. Youth ministers are three times as likely as other ministers, for example, to have taken part in organized youth programs fostering spirituality such as Search, Teens Encounter Christ or Antioch, either as participants or leaders. Nine times out of ten they also served first as volunteers in parishes before being offered paid positions. But volunteerism prior to ministry is not particular to youth ministers. It appears as a general trend in all ministry positions and, interestingly, may account for the greater number of lay women in ministry.

Paths to Ministry

The most common way pastors who employ lay ministers recruit staff is through and among people they know, people whose work they've seen or have heard about through a colleague. Eighty percent report using this method and quite often the people they hire are parish volunteers. These findings correlate with the experiences of lay ministers themselves: 44 percent claim one of their three major reasons for entering parish ministry was having been asked to do so by the pastor or some other member of the pastoral staff.

These volunteers who became paid ministers are significantly more likely to be women, according to the survey. This is consistent with findings from the *Notre Dame Study of Catholic Parish Life*[1] where the majority of those participating in parish activities were found to be women: over 80 percent of CCD teachers and sponsors of the catechumenate, 75 percent of those who participate or lead adult Bible studies or religious discussions, 70 percent of those who are active in parish renewal and spiritual growth, and 85 percent of those who lead or assist in programs designed to help the poor, visit the sick, comfort the grieving and minister to the handicapped. Not only were women more active than men, but according to lists compiled by the Notre Dame staff of the "most influential parishioners," the majority of those perceived as parish leaders (58 percent) were women. Given these facts, if pastors continue recruiting volunteers and parish leaders to fill paid positions, it is unlikely the percentage of men in parish ministry will increase. That is, unless men become more active in parish life.

But this is unlikely. Involving men at the parish level is not a strength the overwhelming majority profess. Little more than half of all parish ministers (male and female) feel they have increased male involvement through their ministry, though more than two-thirds feel they have done so for women. Not only is the stereotypical notion of ministerial activity as nurturing and thus the proper domain of women still active among many men (and perhaps women), but parish ministers also evidence a general sense of not knowing how to minister to men. This pertains not only to women: *all* lay ministers (men and women alike) feel this way. Most report the area of parish life they have least improved is "sensitivity to men's concerns." Only about a third feel they have made a contribution in this direction, though more than half --by contrast-- feel they have done so regarding womens' concerns. Perhaps the notion of "men's concerns" is still rather vague --certainly not as well articulated as "women's concerns" in the minds of most-- which would explain the low marks ministers give themselves in this area. Yet there are issues pertinent to men's experience -- issues relating to job, status and one's role in the family-- that need addressing on a pastoral level.

Affording Ministry

We have suggested several factors affecting the involvement of men and women in parish ministry. Yet the economic factor may prove the most important of all.

Wages in ministry are relatively low. Those younger and single with no families and few major financial commitments (who are mostly men) and those married in dual income households (who are mostly women), can sustain themselves relatively well. But when ministry becomes the primary income in a family situation, the situation changes. Take youth ministers for example. Of those 35 or younger 85 percent are men, three-fourths of whom are unmarried. However, about the time most youth ministers would have married and started families, making their income more important (mid-thirties on), men are noticeably absent. It is during this period that the proportion of women in youth ministry increases exponentially. Over the age of 35, about 82 percent of youth ministers are women, nearly two-thirds of whom are married. Their pay is a second income.

What is true of youth ministers appears true of all lay ministers, though to a lesser degree. Excluding youth ministers one finds that the majority of men (52 percent) are 35 years or younger, most (69 percent) of whom are single. The majority of women (87 percent) are over the age of 35, most (59 percent) of whom are married. These figures do not irrefutably prove, but do strongly suggest, that issues of financial compensation influence who is in ministry and reinforce the sentiment that ministry work as a primary income in a family situation is not viable for men or women.

When asked directly to rate the compensation they receive from their work, specifically whether the money they receive meets their personal needs, few lay ministers (about 4 percent) found their compensation "excellent." Most rated their compensation "fair" (43 percent) or "good" (38 percent) while some (15 percent) said "poor." When it came to meeting family needs, lay ministers were less positive in rating their compensation. Though about 4 percent still found it "excellent," fewer found it "fair" (41 percent) or "good" (32 percent) and more rated it "poor" (23 percent). That the majority found their compensation "fair" to "good" in meeting their family needs is somewhat encouraging. But that nearly one in four found their compensation poor suggests there is real need for improvement, for one must keep in mind that these responses tell only half the story: the story of lay parish ministers who have been able to make ends meet. Those who have not have already left ministry (as the demographics suggest). In essence, those in ministry right now are those that can *afford* to be in ministry.

Issues surrounding financial compensation are not only a concern of lay ministers, but of pastors as well, for the costs of hiring lay ministers can be prohibitive. Larger, wealthier parishes find hiring ministers less of a problem due to their substantial resource base. But parishes without such resources find that hiring decisions are often determined by the expense of the minister. Parishes that need full-time lay ministers, but cannot afford to pay the required salary and health benefits, may opt to hire people with health coverage via their spouse, or choose to hire part-time ministers to circumvent health costs. The situations vary, but parish financial constraints are real and in their own way add a twist to what was said earlier: those in ministry right now are those that *parishes can afford* to have in ministry.

The Spiritual Dimension

One area yet unmentioned is the spiritual dimension of ministry, and in this area men and women are more similar than different. For example, when asked to cite their three major reasons for entering church ministry, the two most frequent responses of both men and women were "felt a call to enter into church service" (56 percent) and "wanted to serve people" (54 percent). Clearly those in parish ministry are those responding to a vocation.

These ministers are very devout. Nearly all go to Mass at least once a week (91 percent of men; 97 percent of women), and of those that do at least half go even more frequently. They also report an active prayer life aside from the prayers they lead as part of their ministry, the majority having a "regular routine" of personal prayer that incorporates meditation, scripture reading, devotionals, among other methods. But having a regular routine of prayer appears a more common trait of women (63 percent) than men (54 percent), though the difference is not statistically significant.

Also in terms of spirituality, the vast majority of lay ministers report feeling "very close" or "close" to God, church and parish, but with some differences. Women feel significantly closer to God than men: 89 percent feel "close" or "very close" compared to 79 percent of the men. And in terms of closeness to the church (meaning the Catholic church at large, not the parish church in particular), the men are significantly more divided: while a nearly equal proportion of men and women (69 percent and 71 percent, respectively) feel "very close" or "close" to the church, men are three times more likely to be "not very close" or "not close at all" (19 percent vs. 7 percent for women). More women choose a neutral position. But in evaluating their parish life men and women are in accord. Most (76 percent) feel at least close to the parish where they worship.

To conclude, we should take stock of what we have learned, namely that the profile of lay men differs strongly from that of lay women in terms of age, marital status, outside work experience, education and paths to ministry. The reasons for these differences need further consideration since they shape the face of lay ministry today and have implications for its future. If some guidance of the development of lay ministry is to come about, understanding the dynamics of who is in lay ministry, how they got there, and what enables them to stay is an important first step. To this end, matters relating to recruitment and financial compensation need special attention.

Notes

1. See David C. Legge and Thomas A. Trozzolo, "Participation in Catholic Parish Life: Religious Rites and Parish Activities in the 1980s," Report No. 3 in *Notre Dame Study of Catholic Parish Life*, April, 1985, p. 7.

Appendix B: Study Surveys

Phase I Survey of Parish Composition and Staffing

Phase II Survey of Lay/Religious Parish Ministers

Phase II Survey of Pastors

National Pastoral Life Center
NCCB Study of Lay Ministry

Name of Parish:_____

[ ] Pastor [ ] Administrator_____

Address:_____Phone (___)_____

City/town_____State_____Zip_____

Arch/Diocese_____

I. PARISH CLASSIFICATION *(Please circle or check number of most apt answer)*

A. What is the locale of the parish?

Inner city	1
Urban business area	2
Other locale within city	3
Suburban (incorporated)	4
Exurban (unincorporated)	5
Town (incorporated place of 2,500 to 49,999)	6
Rural or farm (less than 2,500 or open land)	7
Resort area (size fluctuates seasonally)	8

B. What is the canonical status of the parish?

Territorial	1
National	2
Other:_____	3

C. Who is primarily responsible for staffing the parish?

Diocesan clergy	1
Religious clergy	2
Lay administrator	3
Other:_____	

D. How many missions, if any, are affiliated with the parish?_____

E. Does the pastor also serve another institutional assignment? *(Describe, e.g., military bases, prisons, state hospitals, colleges, and indicate % of time spent on that assignment.)*

% of time____ Description:_____

_____

II. POPULATION CHARACTERISTICS

A. Estimate total population (both Catholic and non-Catholic) within the parish boundaries including missions. *(If a national or other personal parish, indicate total related population. Circle each column)*

	Now	5 yrs. ago
under 1,000	1	1
1,000-4,999	2	2
5,000-9,999	3	3
10,000-19,999	4	4
20,000-39,999	5	5
40,000 or more	6	6

B. Estimate portion of total population that would identify themselves as Catholic: *(Circle number)*

1	10% or less
2	11-20%
3	21-40%
4	41-60%
5	61-80%
6	81-100%

Basis for estimate, e.g., census, popular opinion: _____

C. Indicate total number of registered parishioners (individuals not households): _____

D. Average Saturday evening/Sunday Mass attendance: _____

E. What nationalities predominate among parishioners' roots? *(Circle numbers)*

	Most Frequent	Second Most
African	1	1
Asian:	2	2
Specify_____		
French	3	3
German	4	4
Hispanic:	5	5
Specify_____		
Haitian	6	6
Hungarian	7	7
Irish	8	8
Italian	9	9
Polish	10	10
Slovak	11	11
Other_____	12	12

F. How would you characterize the economic status of parishioners?

Poor	____%
Working Class	____%
Middle income	____%
Upper middle income	____%
Upper income	____%
	= 100%

G. Estimate the educational profile of the parishioners:

        College graduates and above   ____%
        High school graduates   ____%
        Some high school education   ____%
        Elementary education or less   ____%
        = 100%

	Number	Average Attendance
H. In a normal weekend (Saturday night, Sunday) how many Masses are celebrated?	_____	_____
In a normal week, how many weekday Masses are celebrated?	_____	_____
In a normal week, how many other formal worship services are conducted (e.g., devotions, other prayer services)?	_____	_____

I. In what percentage of the Masses and other religious services are the following languages used:

      1 English   ____%
      2 French   ____%
      3 German   ____%
      4 Italian   ____%
      5 Polish   ____%
      6 Spanish   ____%
      7 Other_____   ____%

III. STAFF

A. How do you recruit or obtain parish staff? *(Circle each that applies)*

    1   One to one recruiting from people you know
    2   Ads in parish bulletin(s)
    3   Use of diocesan recruiting or clearinghouse
    4   Advertisement in diocesan or other local papers
    5   Advertisement in national papers, publications
    6   Contact with religious orders
    7   Contact colleges, universities, etc.
    8   Other_____

B. Who is responsible for recruiting/hiring? *(Circle number of each who participates)*

    1   Pastor/administrator
    2   Other staff
    3   Parish council members
    4   Other parishioners
    5   Diocesan staff
    6   Religious order staff
    7   Other_____

4

C. Do you have any written employment guidelines, policies? *(Circle each)*

    1   Parish's own guideline/policies
    2   Diocesan guideline/policies
    3   None
            (If yes, we would be very grateful to receive a copy)

D. School and staff

    1. Does the parish have a school or schools?
       Yes ___ No ___ *(If no, skip to item E)*

    2. Is the school supported solely by your parish or is the support consolidated with other parishes?
       ____ Solely by parish   _____ Consolidated with other parishes

    3. Please indicate:

       Range of grades (e.g., K-8, 1-8, etc.)   _____
       Enrollment 1989-1990 (number)   _____
       Enrollment 1984-1985 (number)   _____
       % enrollment **NOT** from within own parish   _____
       % enrollment **NOT** Catholic   _____

E. Does the diocese provide any special training for pastoring/administration? *(Check one)*

                                   Time Spent in Program
    ____ A Voluntary Program(s)   _____ Days
    ____ Mandatory Program(s)   _____ Days
    ____ None

F. Are there diocesan ministerial continuing education events? *(Check each)*

    ____ For priests only
    ____ Occasionally for both priests and other pastoral ministers
    ____ Frequently for both priests and other pastoral ministers
    ____ For non-ordained pastoral ministers only
    ____ None

G. If the parish is staffed by a religious order, do other members who live in the house participate in the pastoral ministry?

    No ____ Yes (number) ____ Other: Explain_____

H. Information about the pastor/administrator

    1) Is this your first time as pastor/administrator? ___Yes ___No

    2) Years as pastor/administrator in this parish? _____

    3) Do you have any experience in diocesan or religious community office work?___No ___Yes Specify position(s)_____

       Total length of time in diocesan or religious community office: _____years

    4) Any other experience in office work?_____

5) Academic Degrees
　　Degree:_____Subject:_____

　　Degree:_____Subject:_____

6) Total <u>number of days</u> given to workshops/courses related to your work other than for degrees in last five years? *(Enter number of days)*

_____Diocesan (or religious order) mandatory
_____Diocesan (or religious order) voluntary
_____College/university/seminary
_____Other local
_____Regional or national

Content: *(Check all that apply)*
_____Theology/scripture
_____Canon law
_____Spirituality *(aside from retreats)*
_____Psychological/personal development *(incl. Myers/Briggs etc)*
_____Organizational development/administration
_____Personnel management/staff development
_____Financial leadership *(budgeting, fund-raising, etc.)*
Other_____

I. Paid Staff *(see pp. 6-7)*

J. Volunteer staff
Please indicate the names and responsibilities of all those who devote an average of 15 or more hours a week to the work of the parish but who are <u>not paid</u>.

Name	Avg. Hrs. Per Week	Primary Functions
1.		
2.		
3.		
4.		
5.		
6.		
7.		
8.		
9.		
10.		

K. Does the parish have regular office hours within which parishioners are expected to make their appointments?_____Yes _____No

L. Does the parish use a phone answering machine/answering service? _____Yes _____No

I. Pastor and Support staff (salary or stipend), beginning with yourself.

Please list by name, beginning with pastor/administrator, each salaried or stipended member of the parish staff including any school staff, and indicate position (e.g. pastor, DRE, pastoral associate, etc.), their years on staff, status (priest, deacon, sister, brother, lay person), salary or stipend annual amount, other costs, approximate number of hours per week for each, and whether or not each is a registered parishioner. Include pastoral and support staff. (All information will be kept confidential.)

Name	Position	Yrs. on staff in any role	Written Job Description (Y-N)
*1.			
2.			
3.			
4.			
5.			
6.			
7.			
8.			
9.			
10.			
11.			
12.			
13.			
14.			
15.			
16.			
17.			
18.			

Use additonal sheets if necessary

*Please use these numbers of each of the staff members to answer questions F. and H. on page 6 and 7.

PERSONNEL COSTS

Annual Salary	Total Other Annual Costs	Status (Sister, Priest, etc.)	Hrs per week	Parishioner? (Y or N)	FOR OFFICE USE ONLY

M. How often, if at all, are there general staff meetings? *(Check one)*

_____ Weekly
_____ Every two-three weeks
_____ Monthly
_____ Occasionally
_____ Never

Which people listed in II.I pp. 6-7 attend general staff meetings? *(Enter the line number of each, e.g., 1, 4, 5, 6, 8, 14)* _____

Do any unpaid volunteers attend general staff meetings? If yes, list type of people, e.g., parish council chair, finance council chair, president of auxiliary.

_____

N. How often are there formal evaluations of staff members?

Persons evaluated:
(Use numbers from II.I pages 6-7)

1 More than once a year   _____
2 Annually   _____
3 Occasionally   _____
4 Never   _____

Who participate in conducting evaluations? (Use numbers from II.I pages 6-7 to indicate persons being evaluated)

1 Pastor/administrator for _____
2 Other staff for _____
3 Pastoral council members for _____
4 Finance council members for _____
5 Other parishioners for _____
6 Diocesan staff for _____
7 Religious order staff for _____
8 Other _____

O. Describe the pastoral staff as a group? *(Circle the number closest to each concept)*

Team	1 2 3 4 5 6 7 8 9 10	Staff
Co-workers	1 2 3 4 5 6 7 8 9 10	Friends
Collaborative	1 2 3 4 5 6 7 8 9 10	Work independently
Serious	1 2 3 4 5 6 7 8 9 10	Light hearted
Laid-back	1 2 3 4 5 6 7 8 9 10	Constant initiative
Quite organized	1 2 3 4 5 6 7 8 9 10	Casual
Liberal	1 2 3 4 5 6 7 8 9 10	Conservative

P. What appears to be the attitude of diocesan leadership regarding religious and lay persons as pastoral ministers (aside from schools)?

    _____Strongly encourage and promote this
    _____Mildly support this
    _____Attitude not clear at all
    _____Opposed

IV. PARISH LIFE

A. Annual number of 1989:

    Infant baptisms _____
    Adult initiation _____
    Marriages _____
    % mixed _____
    Funerals _____

B. How many participate in religious education programs outside the parochial school? *(Enter number)*

    Elementary grades _____
    High school grades _____
    Adult religious education _____

C. Does the parish use the following:
    Catechumenate (RCIA)   __ Yes __ No

- -

    Communal penance   __ Yes __ No
    Number of times a year _____
    Average number participating _____

- -

    Communal anointing   __ Yes __ No
    Number of times a year _____
    Average number participating _____

D. Does the parish provide in any special way for the disabled? __ No __ Yes

    Describe: _____

    _____

E. Have you undergone any formal planning process for the parish? __ No __ Yes
If yes, please describe:_____

F. Does the parish have a written mission statement?
    _____No _____Yes (if yes, please send copy)

G. For which of the following does the parish have a formally organized program to which some staff time is regularly devoted? *(Check yes or no)*

	Yes	No
1 Liturgy planning group	___	___
2 Youth ministry program	___	___
3 Young adult ministry program	___	___
4 Marriage and family development program	___	___
5 Social services: organized ways to meet individual needs	___	___

- -

	Yes	No
6 Social action: organized groups to effect change or for social justice education	___	___
7 Evangelization (e.g.,_____)	___	___
8 Charismatic prayer group	___	___
9 Ministry to separated/divorced	___	___
10 Ministry to the elderly	___	___

- -

	Yes	No
11 Musical, drama or other cultural activities	___	___
12 Choir, liturgical support group	___	___
13 Program for visitation, care of sick, shut-ins	___	___
14 Ministry training program	___	___
15 12 step programs (AA, NA, ACOA, etc.) List which_____	___	___

- -

	Yes	No
16 Periodic parish mission	___	___
17 RENEW or other parish renewal programs: _____	___	___
18 Bereavement ministry	___	___
19 Picnic, pot luck supper or other social events for whole parish	___	___
20 Bingo, night at the races, raffles, etc.	___	___

- -

	Yes	No
21 Every-home visitation program	___	___
22 Ecumenical activity	___	___

23 Other _____

H. Please check which adult programs the parish sponsors: *(Indicate numbers participating, and briefly describe)*

Check		Nos.	Description
_____	Ad hoc lectures	___	_____
_____	Lecture series	___	_____
_____	Scripture study group(s)	___	_____
_____	Other ongoing small group(s)	___	_____

Is there a local retreat house, college, or some other local institution where your parishioners receive adult religious education? If yes, describe it and indicate how many of your parishioners participate.

_____

_____

I. For which of the following, if any, does the parish have a special program for training parish leadership or ministers? *(Check those that apply)*

_____ Lectors   _____ Family ministers
_____ Eucharistic ministers   _____ Youth minister
_____ Council members   _____ Small group leaders
_____ Social ministry
Other_____

J. Have you used any formal staff development processes or consultants? ____Yes ____No
If yes, please describe.

_____

_____

K. What events, programs, policies, structures or practices of the parish have most enhanced parish life? *(List in order of impact)*

1._____

2._____

3._____

4._____

5._____

L. Any events, policies, etc., that have been a source of friction?

1._____

2._____

3._____

4._____

5._____

M. Do you have a parish photo directory of parishioners? _____Yes _____No

V. FINANCES

A. Has the parish promoted tithing, other forms of stewardship, or an annual pledge?

_____ Yes (Describe):_____

Percent registered parishioners participating financially: _____ %
Percent of parishioners giving time: _____%

_____ No

12

B. Income: *(1988-89 year or 1989 if using calendar year)*

1. Total offertory, tithing, general income $ _____
2. Total bingo, other general fund raising income $ _____
3. Total special appeal income, e.g., capital campaign $ _____
4. Total income from school tuition and other school fund raising $ _____
5. Total subsidy TO the parish $ _____
6. Other general parish income (do not include special
   diocesan or national collections, cemetery income,
   or other income intended for other purposes) $ _____
7. Total parish income $ _____
8. Percent change from 1987-1988 + _____ %
   - _____ %

C. Expenses

1. Total general parish expenses $ _____
2. Total school expenses (for own school or for
   parishioners in other schools) $ _____
3. Total parish contribution to other churches or
   charities (e.g., tithe, twinning etc.) $ _____
4. Total special capital expenses (related to special
   appeal above) $ _____
5. Total diocesan support (including cathedraticum, school
   tax, etc. not annual or special diocesan appeal) $ _____
6. Other expenses $ _____

7. Total expenses $ _____
8. Percent change from 1987-1988 + _____ %
   - _____ %

Thank you very much for your cooperation.

**If we need your parish for the second stage of this study of laity and religious in parish ministry, can we count on your cooperation?
[ ] Yes [ ] No**

Please mail in return envelope enclosed to: NCCB Lay Ministry Study, National Pastoral Life Center, 299 Elizabeth Street, New York, NY 10012-2806

NATIONAL STUDY
OF
LAY AND RELIGIOUS
PARISH MINISTERS

NATIONAL CONFERENCE OF CATHOLIC BISHOPS

NATIONAL PASTORAL LIFE CENTER
299 ELIZABETH STREET
NEW YORK, NY 10012
(212) 431-7825

SURVEY FORM FOR:

LAY OR RELIGIOUS
PARISH MINISTER

Survey Code: _____

Name _____ Title _____

Parish _____

Address _____

City, State, Zip _____

Phone (____)_____ Arch/Diocese _____

Dear Participant:

Welcome! Your parish has been chosen by a random sampling process to be a participant in a national study that seeks to understand better what helps and what hinders the work of lay persons and religious in full-time parish ministry.

This study, commissioned by the National Conference of Catholic Bishops, is being conducted by the National Pastoral Life Center.

The purpose is to study the emerging relationships among clergy, religious and laity, the new roles, responsibilities and procedures now evolving, and the apparent effectiveness of these ministers as perceived by themselves and by knowledgeable observers in the parish.

Surveys will be filled out by the lay and religious ministers, pastors and other ordained staff, and parishioners in parishes in 43 dioceses across the country.

Results will provide a profile of current church experience, identify factors that contribute to a better integration, and suggest recommendations for enhancing further development.

Therefore, your cooperation and contribution in this study is of vital importance.

We ask that you return your survey directly to us in the enclosed self-addressed stamped envelope AS SOON AS POSSIBLE, or at the latest by February 15, 1991.

A limited number of site visits will be made to a select number of parishes after this phase of the study, and so we ask that you identify yourself and your parish. However, be assured that the CONFIDENTIALITY of your responses will be respected and ANONYMITY will be ensured.

We appreciate your time and interest, and thank you for working with us on this national study.

DIRECTIONS

This survey is divided into several sections. Directions for answering each question are clearly marked, and consist mostly of _circling the letter_ of the chosen response from a number of possible answers, or selecting a letter or number from a list of possible answers and _writing this number or letter_ on the appropriate line. Where comments are requested, we ask that you print or write as legibly as possible with a black or blue pen. We value your comments.

AGAIN, THANK YOU.

I. BACKGROUND INFORMATION

Please circle a single number or letter for your answer unless otherwise indicated.

1. What is the year of your birth? _____

2. What is your gender?
   a. Female   b. Male

3. In which group do you belong?
   a. White
   b. Black
   c. Hispanic (Mexican, Puerto Rican, Cuban or other Spanish background)
   d. Asian/Pacific Islander
   e. North American Indian, Alaskan native
   f. Other, please explain: _____

4. Information on Baptism: *(circle one)*
   a. I was baptized Roman Catholic as a child
   b. I became a Catholic later
   c. I am a baptized member of another Christian church
   d. I was never baptized

5. Please circle your status:
   a. Married
   b. Widowed
   c. Divorced and annulled
   d. Divorced, no annulment
   e. Separated
   f. Single (never married)

6. Are you: *(circle one)*
   a. Lay person
   b. Religious sister
   c. Religious brother
   d. Former religious
   e. Inactive priest

7. Were you formerly employed full-time in a field other than church ministry?
   a. Yes   b. No

8. If YES: *(circle the most recent applicable response)*

   a. Professional in a profit corporation
   b. Professional in a non-profit corporation (including public service)
   c. Support staff in a profit corporation
   d. Support staff in a non-profit corporation (including public service)

1

Here are some reasons why persons enter church ministry:

    A. Invitation by the pastor or other parish leader
    B. Example of other parish leaders
    C. Encouragement by family
    D. Encouragement by religious sisters or brothers
    E. To help my spiritual life
    F. Wanted to be part of a religious community
    G. To draw closer to God
    H. Felt called to enter into church service
    I. Wanted to be a part of church life in a more active way
    J. Wanted to serve people
    K. The job fit my needs
    L. Other, please explain:_____

        _____

Based on the above list, rank the **THREE MAJOR REASONS** *why you entered church ministry by writing the appropriate* <u>letter</u> *in the following spaces:*

9. First major reason: _____

10. Second major reason: _____

11. Third major reason: _____

Here are some movements or organizations. Circle **P** *and/or* **L** *if you have been involved as a participant and/or leader in the following:*

	Movement/Organization	Participant	Leader
12.	Marriage Encounter	P	L
13.	Charismatic Renewal	P	L
14.	Cursillo	P	L
15.	Christian Family Movement	P	L
16.	Search, TEC, or Antioch	P	L
17.	RENEW	P	L
18.	Other: _____	P	L

19. Have you served as a volunteer in parishes prior to becoming a full-time minister?
        a. Yes   b. No

20. Please circle the highest education level you have achieved:
        a. Less than a high school graduate
        b. High school graduate
        c. Vocational school beyond high school
        d. Some college
        e. College graduate
        f. Some graduate work
        g. M.A., M.S. or M.Ed.
        h. M.Div.
        i. D.Min.
        j. Ph.D. or Ed.D.

21. Please circle the major field of your highest degree:
- a. Theology
- b. Religious education
- c. Pastoral ministry
- d. Education
- e. Business
- f. Counselling/psychology
- g. Liberal arts
- h. Social work
- i. Social sciences
- j. Music
- k. Liturgy
- l. Administration
- m. Other:_____

21A. If you have a second degree equivalent to your highest, please circle the major field:
- a. Theology
- b. Religious education
- c. Pastoral ministry
- d. Education
- e. Business
- f. Counselling/psychology
- g. Liberal arts
- h. Social work
- i. Social sciences
- j. Music
- k. Liturgy
- l. Administration
- m. Other:_____

22. How many years did you attend Catholic school? _____ years

23. Have you participated in any formal, non-degree educational or training programs related to your current ministry?
- a. Yes
- b. No

If you answered __YES__ to question 23, please answer questions 24 through 29. If you answered __NO__ to question 23, please skip to question 30.

Regarding the training program where you spent the greatest amount of time, please answer these questions:

24. Using the list of fields in *question 21*, what was the field of this program: *(write the letter)* _____

25. Who was the sponsor of this program?
- a. Diocese
- b. Seminary
- c. University
- d. Professional Organization
- e. Parish

26. Did this program lead to certification?
- a. Yes
- b. No

If you attended another non-degree educational or training program related to your current ministry, please answer these questions:

27. Using the list of fields in *question 21*, what was the field of this program: *(write the letter)* _____

28. Who was the sponsor of this program?
- a. Diocese
- b. Seminary
- c. University
- d. Professional organization
- e. Parish

29. Did this program lead to certification?
        a. Yes   b. No

30. Aside from the parish you listed on *the front cover*, are you employed by another church institution?
        a. Yes   b. No

31. If you answered <u>YES</u> to *question 30*, specify the type of institution by circling the letter of appropriate response. If you answered <u>NO</u> to *question 30*, skip to *question 33*.
        a. A diocesan office
        b. Another parish
        c. Some other institution (specify): _____

32. How many hours per week do you work in this other employment? _____ *hours*

33. Which of the following periodicals do you read regularly? *(circle the letter of all applicable)*

a. America	n. Mensaje
b. The Catechist	o. Pastoral Music
c. Catechumenate	p. Praying
d. Chicago Studies	q. Salt
e. Church	r. Sojourners
f. Commonweal	s. St. Anthony's Messenger
g. Crux of the News	t. Theological Studies
h. Homiletic & Pastoral Review	u. Twin Circle
i. Living Light	v. U.S. Catholic
j. National Catholic Register	w. The Wanderer
k. National Catholic Reporter	x. Revista Maryknoll
l. Origins	y. Your diocesan newspaper
m. Our Sunday Visitor	z. Other: _____

II. RELIGIOUS ATTITUDES AND SPIRITUAL EXPERIENCES

Please look at the circle. The rings are meant to show how close or distant you feel in certain relationships. The inside circle - 1 - stands for "Very close." The outside circle - 5 - stands for "Not at all close." The other circles stand for in-between. For each relationship shown below, please show what numbered ring best represents how close you feel. (Circle one number beside each phrase)

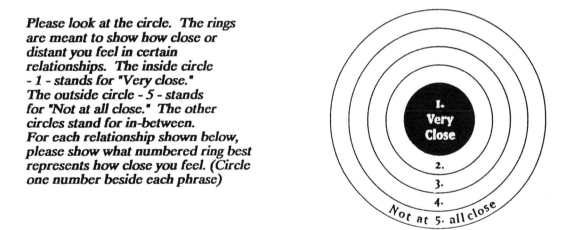

		Very close				Not at all close
1.	How close do you feel to God most of the time?	1	2	3	4	5
2.	How close did you feel to God five years ago?	1	2	3	4	5

4

3. How close do you feel today to
   the Catholic Church?   1   2   3   4   5

4. How close did you feel to the
   Catholic Church five years ago?   1   2   3   4   5

5. How close do you feel today to
   the parish where you worship?   1   2   3   4   5

6. How close did you feel to the
   parish where you worshipped five   1   2   3   4   5
   years ago?

7. Please circle the number on the continuum which describes the religious behavior of your family when
   you were growing up.

   Very religious   1   2   3   4   5   **Not religious**

8. Do you usually worship at the parish where you work?
   a. Yes   b. No

9. Which characteristics best describe your own personal prayer life, aside from the prayers you lead as
   part of your ministry? *(circle one)*
   a. Regular routine
   b. Erratic pattern
   c. Seldom apart from the prayer activities of my ministry

10. How often do you participate in a eucharistic liturgy or a communion service?
    a. Daily
    b. Several times a week
    c. Weekly
    d. Several times a month
    e. Monthly
    f. Several times a year
    g. Less than several times a year

11. Which forms of prayer do you use? *(circle all applicable)*
    a. Liturgy of the Hours
    b. Meditation
    c. Scripture reading
    d. Devotional, including the rosary
    e. Other forms of prayer. Specify: _____

       _____

12. How often do you go on retreats?
    a. Annually
    b. Occasionally
    c. Never

*Parish ministers can have different emphases for their ministry. Though you may feel that each or all of the following objectives are important for your ministry, for each question circle the number closest to that which indicates which is more important to you for **your** work in parish ministry.*

13.	Involvement of people in the church	1	2	3	4	5	Fostering people's relation to God
14.	Encouraging expression of personal belief and exercise of individual conscience	1	2	3	4	5	Conveying authentic church teaching
15.	Fostering sacramental participation	1	2	3	4	5	Fostering private prayer
16.	Being a minister of the gospel	1	2	3	4	5	Being a minister of the church

III. MINISTRY PREPARATION AND EXPERIENCE

1. Have you previously been employed as a church minister? *(circle all applicable)*
    a. Yes, as a parish school teacher, principal or administrator
    b. Yes, in some other school ministry
    c. Yes, in some other form of parish ministry
    d. Yes, in some other church institution
    e. No

2. If you answered <u>NO</u> to *question 1*, skip to *question 4*. If you answered <u>YES</u>, how many years were you employed all together? _____ *year(s)*

3. If you previously served elsewhere as a church minister, what is the <u>MAIN REASON</u> you left your last position? *(circle one only)*
    a. Better salary at new position
    b. Family relocation
    c. Change of pastor
    d. Change of principal
    e. Greater responsibilities at new position
    f. Conflict at old position
    g. Wanted to work primarily with adults
    h. Concern for social justice
    i. Concern for mission of the church
    j. Position was discontinued
    k. Wanted a change of ministry
    l. Other, please explain:_____

    _____

4. How many years have you served in your present position? _____ *year(s)*

5. How long do you envision remaining in your present position?
   a. Only for a short time or until the end of my contract
   b. For the foreseeable future
   c. Don't know

6. How long do you envision working for the church?
   a. Only for a short time or until the end of my contract
   b. For the foreseeable future
   c. Don't know

7. How did you **FIRST** learn about your present position of ministry? *(please circle one only)*
   a. National newspaper advertisement
   b. Diocesan newspaper advertisement
   c. Diocesan ministry placement network
   d. National ministry placement network
   e. Diocesan personnel office
   f. Parish advertisement
   g. Word of mouth
   h. Religious order network
   i. Contacted and asked to apply by present parish staff
   j. Came from pastor's previous parish
   k. Other, please explain: _____

   _____

8. What type of professional certification or academic credentials were required for your present position?
   a. Bachelor's degree or equivalent
   b. Master's degree or equivalent
   c. Diocesan certification or special training
   d. None
   e. Other, please explain: _____

IV. WORK CONDITIONS

Given the limitations of the parish, indicate whether each of the following are adequate or inadequate for your work by circling the appropriate letter:

1.	Location of office:	a.	Adequate	b.	Inadequate
2.	Amount of space:	a.	Adequate	b.	Inadequate
3.	Budget:	a.	Adequate	b.	Inadequate
4.	Privacy of work area:	a.	Adequate	b.	Inadequate
5.	Secretarial help:	a.	Adequate	b.	Inadequate
6.	Meeting space:	a.	Adequate	b.	Inadequate
7.	Room for meals/breaks:	a.	Adequate	b.	Inadequate
8.	Access to professional publications:	a.	Adequate	b.	Inadequate
9.	Office equipment:	a.	Adequate	b.	Inadequate

V. THE EMERGING RELATIONSHIPS AMONG PRIESTS, RELIGIOUS, AND LAITY WHEN SERVING TOGETHER ON PARISH STAFFS

Please look at the circles.
The rings are meant to show how close or distant you feel in certain relationships. The inside circle - 1 - stands for "Very close." The outside circle - 5 - stands for "Not close at all." The other circles stand for in-between. For each relationship you have with the following members of your parish staff, circle the number that best identifies the quality of that relationship. Circle number 6 ("Mixed experience") or number 7 ("Not applicable") if this is the best way to describe the experience.

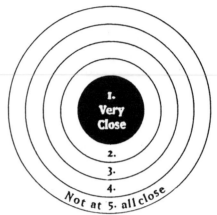

	Staff members	Very close			Not close at all		Mixed exper-ience	Not appli-cable
1.	Pastor	1	2	3	4	5	6	7
2.	Other priests	1	2	3	4	5	6	7
3.	Deacons	1	2	3	4	5	6	7
4.	Sisters	1	2	3	4	5	6	7
5.	Brothers	1	2	3	4	5	6	7
6.	Lay women	1	2	3	4	5	6	7
7.	Lay men	1	2	3	4	5	6	7
8.	School principal	1	2	3	4	5	6	7

Efforts and forms of collaboration, cooperation and team work are experienced in a variety of ways. Below is a list of possible parish staff activities. For each of the following, circle the number on the continuum that best describes how important each activity is to you, whether it is part of your present practice or not:

		Very important			Not at all important	
9.	Staff meetings	1	2	3	4	5
10.	Staff prayer (over and above meetings)	1	2	3	4	5
11.	Socializing with staff (outside of work)	1	2	3	4	5
12.	Staff work retreats (overnights or special full days)	1	2	3	4	5
13.	Staff spiritual days of recollection or retreats	1	2	3	4	5

Regarding parish staff activities, please circle the response that best describes your present parish staff experience.

14. Staff meetings:
    a. We have them at least a few times a month
    b. We have them occasionally
    c. We don't have them

15. Prayer with the staff over and above meetings:
    a. We do this regularly
    b. We do this occasionally
    c. We don't do this

16. Socializing with other staff members:
    a. We do this as a group, at least occasionally
    b. Individuals do this
    c. We don't do this

17. Staff work retreats (overnights or special full days):
    a. We do this regularly
    b. We do this occasionally
    c. We don't do this

18. Staff spiritual days of recollection or retreats:
    a. We do this regularly
    b. We do this occasionally
    c. We don't do this

19. Regarding working styles: *(circle only one)*
    a. We work together on most ministries of the parish
    b. We cooperate and keep fully aware of each other's work,
        but each is basically responsible for her/his own work
    c. We each tend to work on our own

20. Regarding decisions: *(circle only one)*
    a. The pastoral members of the staff make most major decisions
        together with the parish council
    b. The pastoral members of the staff make most major decisions jointly
    c. Each makes decisions in her/his area of parish life with the pastor
    d. Each makes decisions in her/his area of parish life independently
    e. The pastor makes most major decisions
    f. Other, please explain:_____

    _____

21. Regarding communications: *(circle only one)*
    a. There is full and open communication among all staff members
    b. The pastor and each staff member try to keep in communication
    c. Communication among members of the staff is very limited

Regarding support, by which of the following do you feel adequately supported?
Please answer __YES__ or __NO__ by circling the appropriate letter.

	Feel adequately supported	
	Yes	No
22. Pastor	Y	N
23. Other ordained staff	Y	N
24. Lay persons on staff	Y	N
25. Religious on staff	Y	N
26. Parish council/leadership	Y	N
27. Parishioners in general	Y	N

28. Which of the following best characterizes the way you work with the pastor?
    a. Team member
    b. Staff member
    c. Colleague
    d. Employee
    e. Helper
    f. Friend

VI. THE STRUCTURE OF PARISH MANAGEMENT

1. Do you have a written job description?
    a. Yes, and I helped write it
    b. Yes, and it was given to me
    c. No

2. Do you have a written job contract?
    a. Yes   b. No

3. Do you receive a formal performance evaluation at least every year?
    a. Yes   b. No

4. Do you regularly meet with your supervisor to review your job performance?
    a. Yes   b. No

5. Are you given sufficient authority to carry out your responsibilities?
    a. Yes   b. No

6. If you answered <u>YES</u> to question 5, skip to question 7. If you answered <u>NO</u>, circle the letter of the response denoting the main reason why you are *not* given sufficient authority to carry out your responsibilities? *(please circle only one)*
    a. Lack of finances
    b. Lack of understanding by others of my role
    c. Restrictions in church law
    d. Restrictions by the pastor
    e. Other, please explain: _____

7. Is there a special budget for your ministry other than your salary and benefits?
    a. Yes   b. No

8. Do you feel free to discuss difficulties and differences of opinion with your supervisor?
    a. Yes   b. No

VII. ACTIVITIES IN MINISTRY

Indicate your level of regular responsibility regarding each of the following ministry areas in your parish by circling the appropriate response.

Ministry	Leader	Take part	Not part of my responsibility	Parish does not have
1. Liturgy planning/development	1	2	3	4
2. Liturgical music: performing/conducting	1	2	3	4
3. Liturgy leadership	1	2	3	4
4. Catechumenate	1	2	3	4
5. Religious education (children/youth/adults)	1	2	3	4

6. Prayer/reflection: small groups	1	2	3	4
7. Youth/young adult ministry	1	2	3	4
8. Marriage preparation	1	2	3	4
9. Ministry to separated/divorced	1	2	3	4
10. Counselling	1	2	3	4
11. Social service (meeting individual needs)	1	2	3	4
12. Social action (action for change)	1	2	3	4
13. Evangelization	1	2	3	4
14. Home visiting	1	2	3	4
15. Ministry to bereaved	1	2	3	4
16. Ministry to the elderly	1	2	3	4
17. 12-step program	1	2	3	4
18. Care of the sick	1	2	3	4
19 Ministry training	1	2	3	4
20. Administration - organizing	1	2	3	4
21. Parish fund raising	1	2	3	4
22. Finance/building management	1	2	3	4

Below is a list of ministry activities that may be a part of your work. If so, based on your training, were you adequately prepared to carry-out these activities and do you perform them well? Answer YES or NO in each column by circling the appropriate letter.

If part of my work:

Activities	Part of my work	Adequately prepared	Perform well
23. Administrating	Y N	Y N	Y N
24. Building community	Y N	Y N	Y N
25. Collaborating	Y N	Y N	Y N
26. Communicating one-on-one	Y N	Y N	Y N
27. Communicating to public groups (i.e., speaking, writing)	Y N	Y N	Y N
28. Counselling	Y N	Y N	Y N
29. Hospitality	Y N	Y N	Y N
30. Leading/co-leading prayer	Y N	Y N	Y N
31. Managing conflict	Y N	Y N	Y N
32. Motivating involvement	Y N	Y N	Y N
33. Organizing projects	Y N	Y N	Y N
34. Performing (musically)	Y N	Y N	Y N
35. Planning	Y N	Y N	Y N
36. Preaching	Y N	Y N	Y N
37. Preparing liturgies	Y N	Y N	Y N
38. Spiritual directing	Y N	Y N	Y N
39. Supervising others	Y N	Y N	Y N
40. Teaching (content)	Y N	Y N	Y N
41. Training (skills)	Y N	Y N	Y N
42. Visiting (i.e., homes, hospitals)	Y N	Y N	Y N

Which of the following content areas are important for your work in the parish and how well prepared do you feel in each? Answer YES or NO in each column by circling the appropriate letter.

Content area	Important to my work		Adequately prepared	
43. Scripture	Y	N	Y	N
44. Doctrine	Y	N	Y	N
45. Moral theology	Y	N	Y	N
46. Liturgy	Y	N	Y	N
47. Spirituality	Y	N	Y	N
48. Family life	Y	N	Y	N
49. Social services	Y	N	Y	N
50. Justice concerns	Y	N	Y	N
51. Youth development	Y	N	Y	N
52. Elderly concerns	Y	N	Y	N

Which of the following activities do you think you ought to be able to do or share in doing in your present position? Which do you actually do? Answer YES or NO in each column by circling the appropriate letter.

Activity	I should do		I do	
53. Preside at weddings	Y	N	Y	N
54. Do marriage preparation	Y	N	Y	N
55. Conduct wake services	Y	N	Y	N
56. Have some lead role at the eucharist	Y	N	Y	N
57. Control some of the budget	Y	N	Y	N
58. Hire staff	Y	N	Y	N
59. Take part in parish council meetings	Y	N	Y	N
60. Relate directly to diocesan offices	Y	N	Y	N
61. Visit parish homes	Y	N	Y	N
62. Take part in the work of the parish school	Y	N	Y	N
63. Lead prayer services	Y	N	Y	N
64. Preach	Y	N	Y	N
65. Preside at funeral services	Y	N	Y	N
66. Other: _____	Y	N	Y	N

67. How many hours do you work each week in your parish position? _____ *hours*

Answer questions 68 through 70 by rating the compensation you receive for your work.

68. The amount of money that you receive to meet your personal needs:
     a. Excellent
     b. Good
     c. Fair
     d. Poor

69. The amount of money you receive to meet your family or congregational family needs:
     a. Excellent
     b. Good
     c. Fair
     d. Poor

70. The amount of pay you receive in comparison to other workers in your area:
    a. Excellent
    b. Good
    c. Fair
    d. Poor

71. To what extent is there a conflict between the time demands of your present ministry and the time required for yourself and your family or religious community?
    a. No significant conflict
    b. Some conflict
    c. A great deal of conflict

72. Do you find it difficult to participate in evening and weekend activities?
    a. Yes   b. No

73. Does the parish provide housing for you?
    a. Yes   b. No

74. Does the parish provide a car and/or mileage reimbursement for the use of your own car?
    a. Yes   b. No

Think of your present working situation. What is it like most of the time? After each word below, circle the response that best describes your work using the code below:
Y - if it describes your work
N - if it does not describe your work

75. Fascinating	Y	N
76. Routine	Y	N
77. Satisfying	Y	N
78. Boring	Y	N
79. Good	Y	N
- -		
80. Creative	Y	N
81. Respected	Y	N
82. Tiresome	Y	N
83. Challenging	Y	N
84. Frustrating	Y	N
- -		
85. Gives sense of accomplishment	Y	N
86. Spiritually rewarding	Y	N

87. Is there a grievance procedure in your parish or diocese?
    a. Yes   b. No

88. In your present position, to whom do you report?
    a. Pastor
    b. Parish administrator (other than pastor)
    c. Associate pastor
    d. Pastoral associate
    e. Director of religious education
    f. Parish council
    g. Diocesan official, please explain:_____

    _____

    h. Other, please explain:_____

    _____

VIII.   WHAT YOUR MINISTRY ADDS TO PARISH LIFE

Indicate the extent to which your own parish ministry has influenced your parish in the following aspects: (circle the answer that best applies)

	Made it worse	Continued what was there	Some improve-ment	Added consid-erably
1. Deepening parish spirituality	1	2	3	4
2. Ability to reach more parishioners	1	2	3	4
3. Competency in more areas/skills	1	2	3	4
4. Enabling parishioners to feel at home in the parish	1	2	3	4
5. Improvement of liturgy/worship	1	2	3	4
6. Improvement of religious education	1	2	3	4
7. Pastoral care to those with various needs	1	2	3	4
8. Counselling	1	2	3	4
9. Spirit of community	1	2	3	4
10. Outreach to wider community concerns	1	2	3	4
11. Sensitivity to family needs	1	2	3	4
12. Sensitivity to women's concerns	1	2	3	4
13. Sensitivity to men's concerns	1	2	3	4
14 Sensitivity to social justice concerns	1	2	3	4
15. Understanding of lay concerns	1	2	3	4
16. Involvement of women	1	2	3	4
17. Involvement of men	1	2	3	4
18. Involvement of elderly	1	2	3	4
19. Involvement of youth	1	2	3	4
20. Management of parish resources	1	2	3	4
21. Communication within the parish	1	2	3	4
22. General strengthening of parish life	1	2	3	4
23. Staff collaboration	1	2	3	4
24. Parish vision and sense of mission	1	2	3	4
25. Planning	1	2	3	4

26. In general, where in the following continuum would you place the overall climate of your parish?

Very Positive   1   2   3   4   5   **Not positive at all**

27. Do parishioners volunteer when new programs and services are presented?
   a.   Always
   b.   Usually
   c.   Sometimes
   d.   Seldom
   e.   Never

IX. SUPPORT STRUCTURES FOR YOUR MINISTRY

What has been and should be the role of the diocese regarding your placement? Answer YES or NO in each column by circling the appropriate response.

		Diocese does		Diocese should do	
1.	Recruiting lay/religious	Y	N	Y	N
2.	Training lay/religious	Y	N	Y	N
3.	Screening lay/religious	Y	N	Y	N
4.	Certifying lay/religious	Y	N	Y	N
5.	Commissioning lay/religious	Y	N	Y	N
6.	Evaluating lay/religious	Y	N	Y	N
7.	Establishing policies, ministry classifications, salary ranges	Y	N	Y	N
8.	Continuing education	Y	N	Y	N
9.	Inclusion in diocesan events	Y	N	Y	N
10.	Staff training and development	Y	N	Y	N

11. Did your diocese have a formal role in your placement?   a. Yes   b. No

12. If you answered NO to *question 11*, skip to *question 13*. If you answered YES, indicate what types of roles? *(please circle all applicable)*
   - a. Recruiting lay/religious
   - b. Training lay/religious
   - c. Screening lay/religious
   - d. Certifying lay/religious
   - e. Commissioning lay/religious
   - f. Evaluating lay/religious
   - g. Establishing policies, ministry classifications, salary ranges
   - h. Continuing education
   - i. Inclusion in diocesan events
   - j. Staff training and development

13. Which diocesan office, in any of its divisions, has the most responsibility for your ministry? *(please circle only one)*

   - a. Aging
   - b. Catholic Charities
   - c. Catholic schools
   - d. Chancery
   - e. Evangelization
   - f. Family Life
   - g. Finance
   - h. Lay ministry
   - i. Minority ministry
   - j. Personnel (general)
   - k. Personnel (priest)
   - l. Religious education
   - m. Rural life
   - n. Social action
   - o. Worship
   - p. Youth
   - q. No specific office
   - r. Other, please explain:_____

   _____

14. Which diocesan office has been the most helpful in your ministry? *(please circle only one)*

   - a. Aging
   - b. Catholic Charities
   - c. Catholic schools
   - d. Chancery
   - e. Evangelization
   - f. Family Life
   - g. Finance
   - h. Lay ministry
   - i. Minority ministry
   - j. Personnel (general)
   - k. Personnel (priest)
   - l. Religious education
   - m. Rural life
   - n. Social action
   - o. Worship
   - p. Youth
   - q. No specific office
   - r. Other, please explain:_____

   _____

15. In general, regarding lay/religious ministry, the diocesan offices have been:
   a. Sufficiently helpful
   b. Not as helpful as they could be

Do you participate in support groups at any of the following levels? (please circle the appropriate response)

16. Area ministry groups or associations:
   a. Yes   b. No   c. Not applicable

17. Diocesan groups or association:
   a. Yes   b. No   c. Not applicable

18. Regional organizations:
   a. Yes   b. No   c. Not applicable

19. National organizations:
   a. Yes   b. No   c. Not applicable

X.   CONCLUDING REFLECTIONS

Please circle the appropriate response by using this code:

SA - Strongly Agree
A - Agree
N - No Opinion or not sure
D - Disagree
SD - Strongly Disagree

1.	Ministry has been affirming to me	SA	A	N	D	SD
2.	Ministry has allowed me to develop and to use my talents in the service of the church	SA	A	N	D	SD
3.	The persons whom I serve have affirmed my worth	SA	A	N	D	SD
4.	My supervisors in the parish are satisfied with my performance as a minister	SA	A	N	D	SD
5.	Other staff members are satisfied with my performance as a minister	SA	A	N	D	SD
6.	Parishioners are satisfied with my performance as a minister	SA	A	N	D	SD
7.	"Networking" with other ministers has been a personal support to me	SA	A	N	D	SD

8. I would encourage others to enter parish ministry	SA	A	N	D	SD
9. Unless the church becomes more open in some of its policies, there may come a time when I can no longer continue to work for the church	SA	A	N	D	SD
10. There may come a time in the future when I may no longer be able to afford to continue working for the church	SA	A	N	D	SD
11. I feel secure in my position	SA	A	N	D	SD
12. I feel I am part of a thriving community in which many of us are achieving spiritual growth	SA	A	N	D	SD

Here is a list of various things which are part of employment as a parish minister:

A. Spiritual life
B. Working conditions
C. Interactions with clergy
D. Interaction with parishioners
E. Challenging responsibilities
F. Affirmation from superiors
G. Personal satisfaction
H. Salary
I. Benefits
J. Chance for continuing education
K. Support from diocesan office
L. Pride in serving the church
M. Job security

From the above list, rank the **three most satisfying characteristics** *about working at your parish by writing the appropriate letter in the following blanks.*

13. ____
14. ____
15. ____

From the above list, rank the **three things most in need of improvement at your parish** *by writing the appropriate letter in the following blanks.*

16. ____
17. ____
18. ____

Here is a summary list of factors related to lay/religious parish ministry:

    A. Current preparation of lay/religious for parish ministry
    B. Integration of lay/religious ministers into lay/religious parish ministry
    C. Structures and policies for lay/religious ministers
    D. Readiness of priests for lay/religious parish ministers
    E. Readiness of parishioners for lay/religious parish ministers
    F. Current support structures for lay/religious parish ministers

From the above list, rank the **three best developed factors** *affecting lay/religious parish ministry by writing the appropriate letter in the following blanks.*

    19. _____
    20. _____
    21. _____

From the above list, rank the **three factors most in need of improvement** *for the future of lay/religious parish ministry by writing the appropriate letter in the following blanks.*

    22. _____
    23. _____
    24. _____

Any final reflections?

_____

_____

_____

_____

_____

_____

_____

_____

_____

_____

If you have a job discription, please attach a copy.

Thank you. We appreciate your cooperation.

NATIONAL STUDY
OF
LAY AND RELIGIOUS
PARISH MINISTERS

NATIONAL CONFERENCE OF CATHOLIC BISHOPS

NATIONAL PASTORAL LIFE CENTER
299 ELIZABETH STREET
NEW YORK, NY 10012
(212) 431-7825

SURVEY FORM FOR:

PASTOR

Survey Code: _____

Name _____ Title _____

Parish _____

Address _____

City, State, Zip _____

Phone (____)_____ Arch/Diocese _____

Dear Participant:

Welcome! Your parish has been chosen by a random sampling process to be a participant in a national study that seeks to understand better what helps and what hinders the work of lay persons and religious in full-time parish ministry.

This study, commissioned by the National Conference of Catholic Bishops, is being conducted by the National Pastoral Life Center.

The purpose is to study the emerging relationships among clergy, religious and laity, the new roles, responsibilities and procedures now evolving, and the apparent effectiveness of these ministers as perceived by themselves and by knowledgeable observers in the parish.

Surveys will be filled out by the lay and religious ministers, pastors and other ordained staff, and parishioners in parishes in 43 dioceses across the country.

Results will provide a profile of current church experience, identify factors that contribute to a better integration, and suggest recommendations for enhancing further development.

Therefore, your cooperation and contribution in this study is of vital importance.

We ask that you return your survey directly to us in the enclosed self-addressed stamped envelope AS SOON AS POSSIBLE, or at the latest by February 15, 1991.

A limited number of site visits will be made to a select number of parishes after this phase of the study, and so we ask that you identify yourself and your parish. However, be assured that the CONFIDENTIALITY of your responses will be respected and ANONYMITY will be ensured.

We appreciate your time and interest, and thank you for working with us on this national study.

DIRECTIONS

This survey is divided into several sections. Directions for answering each question are clearly marked, and consist mostly of <u>circling the letter</u> of the chosen response from a number of possible answers, or selecting a letter or number from a list of possible answers and <u>writing this number or letter</u> on the appropriate line. Where comments are requested, we ask that you print or write as legibly as possible with a black or blue pen. We value your comments.

AGAIN, THANK YOU.

I. BACKGROUND INFORMATION

Please circle a single number or letter for your answer unless otherwise indicated.

1. What is the year of your birth? _____

2. In which group do you belong?
   a. White
   b. Black
   c. Hispanic (Mexican, Puerto Rican, Cuban or other Spanish background)
   d. Asian/Pacific Islander
   e. North American Indian, Alaskan native
   f. Other, please explain: _____

3. Information on Baptism: *(circle one)*
   a. I was baptized Catholic as a child
   b. I became a Catholic later

4. How many years have you been ordained? _____ year(s)

5. Describe any formal education beyond the seminary:
   a. Some graduate work
   b. M.A., M.S. or M.Ed.
   c. M.Div.
   d. D.Min.
   e. Ph.D.
   f. Other:_____

6. Have you ever held a full-time position as a priest other than parish work?
   a. Yes   b. No

7. If you answered <u>NO</u> to *question 6*, skip to *question 8*. If you answered <u>YES</u>, in what area?
   a. Education (teaching, administration)
   b. Chancery or other diocesan office
   c. Chaplaincy (military, hospital, prison)
   d. Other:_____

8. Which of the following periodicals do you read regularly? *(circle the letter of all applicable)*

a. America	o. Pastoral Music
b. The Catechist	p. Praying
c. Catechumenate	q. The Priest
d. Chicago Studies	r. Salt
e. Church	s. Sojourners
f. Commonweal	t. St. Anthony's Messenger
g. Crux of the News	u. Theological Studies
h. Homiletic & Pastoral Review	v. Twin Circle
i. Living Light	w. U.S. Catholic
j. National Catholic Register	x. The Wanderer
k. National Catholic Reporter	y. Revista Maryknoll
l. Origins	z. Your diocesan newspaper
m. Our Sunday Visitor	aa. Other: _____
n. Mensaje	

9. Does the parish have a parish pastoral council?
   a. Yes
   b. No and never had
   c. Once had, but no longer

1

10. Does the parish have a finance council?
    a. Yes   b. No

II.   RELIGIOUS ATTITUDES AND SPIRITUAL EXPERIENCES

We are asking the lay/religious parish ministers about their own spiritual practices to determine in what ways these affect their ministry. It will help us to interpret their responses if we can compare them with your own practices.

Please look at the circle. The rings are meant to show how close or distant you feel in certain relationships. The inside circle - 1 - stands for "Very close." The outside circle - 5 - stands for "Not at all close." The other circles stand for in-between. For each relationship shown below, please show what numbered ring best represents how close you feel. (Circle one number beside each phrase)

	Very close			Not at all close	
1. How close do you feel to God most of the time?	1	2	3	4	5
2. How close did you feel to God five years ago?	1	2	3	4	5
3. How close do you feel today to the Catholic Church?	1	2	3	4	5
4. How close did you feel to the Catholic Church five years ago?	1	2	3	4	5

5. Which characteristics best describe your own personal prayer life aside from the prayers you lead as part of your ministry? *(circle one)*
    a. Regular routine
    b. Erratic pattern
    c. Seldom apart from the prayer activities of my ministry

6. Which forms of prayer do you use? *(circle all applicable)*
    a. Liturgy of the hours
    b. Meditation
    c. Scripture reading
    d. Devotional, including the rosary
    e. Other forms of prayer. Specify: _____

7. How often do you go on retreats?
    a. Annually
    b. Occasionally
    c. Never

Pastors can have different emphases for their ministry. Though you may feel that each or all of the following objectives are important for your ministry, for each question circle the number closest to that which indicates which is more important to you for your work as a pastor.

8.	Involvement of people in the church	1	2	3	4	5	Fostering people's relation to God
9.	Encouraging expression of personal belief and exercise of individual conscience	1	2	3	4	5	Conveying authentic church teaching
10.	Fostering sacramental participation	1	2	3	4	5	Fostering private prayer
11.	Being a minister of the gospel	1	2	3	4	5	Being a minister of the church

III. THE EMERGING RELATIONSHIPS AMONG PRIESTS, RELIGIOUS, AND LAITY WHEN SERVING TOGETHER ON PARISH STAFFS

Please look at the circles. The rings are meant to show how close or distant you feel in certain relationships. The inside circle - 1 - stands for "Very close." The outside circle - 5 - stands for "Not close at all." The other circles stand for in-between. For each relationship which you have with the following members of your parish staff, circle the number that best identifies the quality of that relationship. Circle number 6 ("Mixed experience") or number 7 ("Not applicable") if this is the best way to describe your experience.

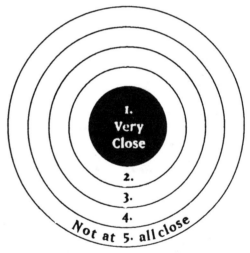

Staff members	Very close			Not close at all		Mixed exper- ience	Not appli- cable
1. Other priests	1	2	3	4	5	6	7
2. Deacons	1	2	3	4	5	6	7
3. Sisters	1	2	3	4	5	6	7
4. Brothers	1	2	3	4	5	6	7
5. Lay women	1	2	3	4	5	6	7
6. Lay men	1	2	3	4	5	6	7
7. School principal	1	2	3	4	5	6	7

In hiring someone for a professional ministry position, how important are the following to you?

8. That the person is lay:
      a. Very important   b. Somewhat important   c. Not important

9. That the person is a parishioner:
      a. Very important   b. Somewhat important   c. Not important

10. That the person is a religious
      a. Very important   b. Somewhat important   c. Not important

11. That the person is male:
      a. Very important   b. Somewhat important   c. Not important

12. That the person is female:
      a. Very important   b. Somewhat important   c. Not important

13. How successful have you been in locating and hiring qualified staff?
      a. We have been able to find qualified people and can pay them fairly
      b. We have been able to find qualified people but have difficulty paying them fairly
      c. We have not been able to find qualified people though we could pay them fairly
      d. We have neither been able to find qualified people nor pay them fairly

Efforts and forms of collaboration, cooperation and team work are experienced in a variety of ways. Below is a list of possible parish staff activities. For each of the following, circle the number on the continuum that best describes how important each activity is to you, whether it is part of your present practice or not:

	Very important			Not at all important	
14. Staff meetings	1	2	3	4	5
15. Staff prayer over and above meetings	1	2	3	4	5
16. Socializing with staff (outside of work)	1	2	3	4	5
17. Staff work retreats (overnights or special full days)	1	2	3	4	5
18. Staff spiritual days of recollection or retreats	1	2	3	4	5

Regarding parish staff activities, please circle the response that best describes your present parish staff experience.

19. Staff meetings:
      a. We have them at least a few times a month
      b. We have them occasionally
      c. We don't have them

20. Prayer with staff over and above meetings:
      a. We do this regularly
      b. We do this occasionally
      c. We don't do this

21. Socializing with other staff members:
      a. We do this as a group, at least occasionally
      b. Individuals do this
      c. We don't do this

22. Staff work retreats (overnights or special full days):
    a. We do this regularly
    b. We do this occasionally
    c. We don't do this

23. Staff spiritual days of recollection or retreats:
    a. We do this regularly
    b. We do this occasionally
    c. We don't do this

24. Regarding working styles: *(circle only one)*
    a. We work together on most ministries of the parish
    b. We cooperate and keep fully aware of each other's work, but each is basically responsible for her/his own work
    c. We each tend to work on our own

25. Regarding decisions: *(circle only one)*
    a. The pastoral members of the staff make most major decisions together with the parish council
    b. The pastoral members of the staff make most major decisions jointly
    c. Each makes decisions in her/his area of parish life with the pastor
    d. Each makes decisions in her/his area of parish life independently
    e. The pastor makes most major decisions
    f. Other, please explain: _____

_____

26. Regarding communications: *(circle only one)*
    a. There is full and open communication among all staff members
    b. The pastor and each staff member try to keep in communication
    c. Communication among members of the staff is very limited

Regarding support, by which of the following do you feel adequately supported? Please answer <u>*YES*</u> *or* <u>*NO*</u> *by circling the appropriate letter.*

Feel adequately supported

	Yes	No
27. Other ordained staff	Y	N
28. Lay persons on staff	Y	N
29. Religious on staff	Y	N
30. Parish council/leadership	Y	N
31. Parishioners in general	Y	N

32. Which of the following best characterizes the way your lay/religious staff works with you?
    a. Team members
    b. Staff members
    c. Colleagues
    d. Employees
    e. Helpers
    f. Friends

Consider your own work as pastor. What is it like most of the time? After each word below, circle the response that best describes your work using the code below:

Y - **if it describes your work**
N - **if it does not describe your work**

33. Fascinating	Y	N	
34. Routine	Y	N	
35. Satisfying	Y	N	
36. Boring	Y	N	
37. Good	Y	N	
38. Creative	Y	N	
39. Respected	Y	N	
40. Tiresome	Y	N	
41. Challenging	Y	N	
42. Frustrating	Y	N	
43. Gives sense of accomplishment	Y	N	
44. Spiritually rewarding	Y	N	

IV. ACTIVITIES OF LAY/RELIGIOUS MEMBER(S) OF STAFF

*Any ministry involves a variety of activities. For example, a person responsible for religious education may sometimes teach, sometimes administrate and sometimes help build parish community. Below is a list of such ministry activities. Do **lay/religious ministers** in your parish perform these activities well? Answer YES or NO in each column by circling the appropriate letter.*

Activities	Part of their work		Perform well	
	Yes	No	Yes	No
1. Administrating	Y	N	Y	N
2. Building community	Y	N	Y	N
3. Collaborating	Y	N	Y	N
4. Communicating one-on-one	Y	N	Y	N
5. Communicating to public groups (i.e., speaking, writing)	Y	N	Y	N
6. Counselling	Y	N	Y	N
7. Hospitality	Y	N	Y	N
8. Leading/co-leading prayer	Y	N	Y	N
9. Managing conflict	Y	N	Y	N
10. Motivating involvement	Y	N	Y	N
11. Organizing projects	Y	N	Y	N
12. Performing (musically)	Y	N	Y	N
13. Planning	Y	N	Y	N
14. Preaching	Y	N	Y	N
15. Preparing liturgies	Y	N	Y	N
16. Spiritual directing	Y	N	Y	N
17. Supervising others	Y	N	Y	N
18. Teaching (content)	Y	N	Y	N
19. Training (skills)	Y	N	Y	N
20. Visiting (i.e., homes, hospitals)	Y	N	Y	N

Which of the following content areas are important for the work of **lay/religious parish ministers** *in your parish and how well prepared do you feel they were regarding each? Answer* <u>YES</u> *or* <u>NO</u> *in each column by circling the appropriate letter.*

Content area	Important to work	Adequately prepared
21. Scripture	Y N	Y N
22. Doctrine	Y N	Y N
23. Moral theology	Y N	Y N
24. Liturgy	Y N	Y N
25. Spirituality	Y N	Y N
26. Family life	Y N	Y N
27. Social services	Y N	Y N
28. Social justice concerns	Y N	Y N
29. Youth development	Y N	Y N
30. Elderly concerns	Y N	Y N

Which of the following activities ought **lay/religious ministers** *be able to do or share in doing in your parish? Which do they actually do? Answer* <u>YES</u> *or* <u>NO</u> *in each column by circling the appropriate letter.*

Activity	They should do	They do
31. Preside at weddings	Y N	Y N
32. Do marriage preparation	Y N	Y N
33. Conduct wake services	Y N	Y N
34. Have some lead role at the eucharist	Y N	Y N
35. Control some of the budget	Y N	Y N
36. Hire staff	Y N	Y N
37. Take part in parish council meetings	Y N	Y N
38. Relate directly to diocesan offices	Y N	Y N
39. Visit parish homes	Y N	Y N
40. Take part in the work of the parish schools	Y N	Y N
41. Lead prayer services	Y N	Y N
42. Preach	Y N	Y N
43. Preside at funeral services	Y N	Y N
44. Other: _____	Y N	Y N

V. WORK CONDITIONS

Given the natural limitations of the parish, what is your opinion of the work conditions of the **lay/religious parish minister(s)?** *Indicate whether each of the following are adequate or inadequate for their work by circling the appropriate letter:*

1. Location of office: a. Adequate   b. Inadequate

2. Amount of space: a. Adequate   b. Inadequate

3. Budget: a. Adequate   b. Inadequate

4. Privacy of work area: a. Adequate   b. Inadequate

5. Secretarial help: a. Adequate   b. Inadequate

		Made it worse	Continued what was there	Some improvement	Added considerably
6.	Meeting space:	a. Adequate	b. Inadequate		
7.	Room for meals/breaks:	a. Adequate	b. Inadequate		
8.	Access to professional publications:	a. Adequate	b. Inadequate		
9.	Office equipment:	a. Adequate	b. Inadequate		

VI. WHAT LAY/RELIGIOUS MINISTRY ADDS TO PARISH LIFE

Indicate the extent to which your **lay/religious parish ministers** *have influenced your parish in the following aspects: (circle the answer that best applies)*

		Made it worse	Continued what was there	Some improvement	Added considerably
1.	Deepening parish spirituality	1	2	3	4
2.	Ability to reach more parishioners	1	2	3	4
3.	Competency in more areas/skills	1	2	3	4
4.	Enabling parishioners to feel at home in the parish	1	2	3	4
5.	Improvement of liturgy/worship	1	2	3	4
6.	Improvement of religious education	1	2	3	4
7.	Pastoral care to those with various needs	1	2	3	4
8.	Counselling	1	2	3	4
9.	Spirit of community	1	2	3	4
10.	Outreach to wider community concerns	1	2	3	4
11.	Sensitivity to family needs	1	2	3	4
12.	Sensitivity to women's concerns	1	2	3	4
13.	Sensitivity to men's concerns	1	2	3	4
14	Sensitivity to social justice concerns	1	2	3	4
15.	Understanding of lay concerns	1	2	3	4
16.	Involvement of women	1	2	3	4
17.	Involvement of men	1	2	3	4
18.	Involvement of elderly	1	2	3	4
19.	Involvement of youth	1	2	3	4
20.	Management of parish resources	1	2	3	4
21.	Communication within the parish	1	2	3	4
22.	General strengthening of parish life	1	2	3	4
23.	Staff collaboration	1	2	3	4
24.	Parish vision and sense of mission	1	2	3	4
25.	Planning	1	2	3	4

26. In general, where in the following continuum would you place the overall climate of your parish?

Very positive 1   2   3   4   5   **Not positive at all**

27. Do parishioners volunteer when new programs and services are presented?
   a. Always
   b. Usually
   c. Sometimes
   d. Seldom
   e. Never

VII. PREPARATION AND SUPPORT FOR LAY/RELIGIOUS PARISH MINISTERS

1. What is your own disposition toward lay/religious parish ministry?
   - a. This is a good development and I feel well prepared for it
   - b. This is a good development but I feel inadequately prepared for it
   - c. This is an unfortunate necessity

What has been and should be the role of the diocese regarding lay parish ministers? Answer <u>YES</u> or <u>NO</u> in each column by circling the appropriate response.

		Diocese does	Diocese should do
2.	Recruiting lay/religious	Y N	Y N
3.	Training lay/religious	Y N	Y N
4.	Screening lay/religious	Y N	Y N
5.	Certifying lay/religious	Y N	Y N
6.	Commissioning lay/religious	Y N	Y N
7.	Evaluating lay/religious	Y N	Y N
8.	Establishing policies, ministry classifications, salary ranges	Y N	Y N
9.	Continuing education of lay/religious	Y N	Y N
10.	Inclusion in diocesan events of lay/religious	Y N	Y N
11.	Staff training and development	Y N	Y N

12. In general, regarding lay/religious ministry, the diocesan offices have been:
    - a. Sufficiently helpful
    - b. Not as helpful as they could be

VIII. CONCLUDING REFLECTIONS

Here is a summary list of factors related to lay/religious parish ministry:

- A. Current preparation of lay/religious for parish ministry
- B. Integration of lay/religious ministers into lay/religious parish ministry
- C. Structures and policies for lay/religious ministers
- D. Readiness of priests for lay/religious parish ministers
- E. Readiness of parishioners for lay/religious parish ministers
- F. Current support structures for lay/religious parish ministers

From the above list, rank the **three best developed factors** *affecting lay/religious parish ministry by writing the appropriate letter in the following blanks.*

1. _____
2. _____
3. _____

From the above list, rank the **three factors most in need of improvement** *for the future of lay/religious parish ministry by writing the appropriate letter in the following blanks.*

4. _____
5. _____
6. _____

Any final reflections?

_____

_____

_____

_____

_____

_____

_____

_____

_____

_____

Thank you. We appreciate your cooperation.

Index